The Necessary Existence of God

The Necessary Existence of God

God

The Proof of Christianity Through PreSuppositional Apologetics

Michael A. Robinson

ISBN : 1-4196-2035-5
Library of Congress Control Number : 2005910405

To order additional copies, please contact us.
BookSurge, LLC
www.booksurge.com
1-866-308-6235
orders@booksurge.com

The Necessary Existence of God

INTRODUCTION

TO KNOW ANYTHING GOD MUST EXIST

Is There a God? Yes!

Rev. Robert H. Tanzie, pastor of the Peace Orthodox Presbyterian Church in Boston, offered this difficulty in an address at Harvard Divinity School: "Many well-intentioned Christians and pagans over the past two millennia have sought to put up...a net [of skepticism] and induce God to pass through it. The effort to construct a rationally transparent test, syllogism, or experiment to prove God's existence to believers and nonbelievers alike is as old as it is futile. [Some] begin with Descartes' 'I think; therefore I am' and [later end] with Bertrand Russell's complaint. When asked what he would say if, after death, he found himself before the Almighty, Professor Russell said he would reply: 'Sir, you did not give me enough proof.'" Pastor Tanzie and Russell are incorrect in assuming that there is no proof. There is certain and absolute proof for the existence of the Triune God, and the proof is the point of this book.

The Alternative: Nothing

The Russian novelist Fyodor Dostoevsky was on to something when he wrote in *The Brothers Karamazov*: "But if we answer the question ["Is there a God?"] in the negative, we must also have the courage to admit the death of man and woman as meaningful and moral beings. If God is dead, then everything is permitted. The exhilaration of freedom from Moses' Ten Commandments, and from Jesus' stern sexual ethic, soon dissipates when we think about the ramifications of our negative answer." Deny God and everything is meaningless and without purpose. But all assertions of meaninglessness are impossible and self-refuting, because if everything is meaningless, so is the very statement that everything is meaningless. There must be meaning. And the meaninglessness that atheism presumes leads only to the atrocities and mass-murders of Stalin and Mao. The old Spanish proverb proves true: "He who goes with wolves learns to howl." Atheism prompted the Communists to "howl" as they butchered millions.

> He is despised and rejected by men, a man of sorrows, and acquainted with grief: and we hid, as it were, our faces from Him; He was despised, and we did not esteem Him. Surely He has borne our griefs and carried our sorrows; yet we esteemed Him stricken, smitten by God, and afflicted. But He was wounded for our transgressions; He was bruised for our iniquities; the chastisement for our peace was upon Him, and by His stripes we are healed. All we like sheep have gone astray; we have turned every one to his own way; And the LORD has laid on Him the iniquity of us all. He was oppressed, and He was afflicted, yet He opened not His mouth; He was led as a lamb to the slaughter, and as a sheep before its shearers is silent, so He opened not His mouth. He was taken from prison and from judgment: and who will declare His generation? For He was cut off from the land of the living; for the transgressions of My people He was stricken. And they made His grave with the wicked—but with the rich at His death, because He had done no violence, nor was any deceit in His mouth. Yet it pleased the LORD to bruise Him; He has put Him to grief. When you make His soul an offering for sin...My righteous Servant shall justify many, for He shall bear their iniquities....And He bore the sin of many, and made intercession for the transgressors (Isaiah 53:3-12).

Those who deny God can do so only because the God of the Bible has given them the reason that makes such a denial possible. As Dutch theologian Cornelius Van Til illustrates, in order for a little child to slap his dad in the face, the child must sit on his father's lap. An unknown author tells the story of a secular psychologist, Jewish by race, who, on hearing the prophecy of Christ's passion and death (Isaiah 52:13-53:12), answered: "What's so impressive about that? Anyone standing at the foot of the cross could have written that." He was amazed to learn that the passage had been written centuries before Jesus' crucifixion. That was the beginning of the end of his secularism. Today that doctor is a Christian.

Sheep have a tendency to grow wool over their eyes. The wool must be trimmed for the sheep to see. And the nonbeliever has a thick cover of wool over his eyes in the form of ungodly intellectual pre-commitments. He cannot see. He is blind and needs the truth of God's revelation to give him sight. We will discover that, without God, nothing can be seen and nothing can make sense.

God is Absolutely Required

The only way to avert skepticism is to have an unchanging, infinite, infallible, and exhaustive authority. The God of the Bible alone has these attributes. God is absolutely required because He is unchanging, universal in knowledge, timeless, transcendent, and nonphysical and the laws of logic are unchanging, universal, timeless, transcendent, and nonphysical. Logic is necessary for all assertions, investigations, and evidence, hence God alone provides the necessary preconditions to make sense of our world and experience. The Triune God must exist, the contrary is impossible.

God is the precondition for intellectual certainty. And there must be certainty. The statement that asserts that there is no certainty is self-refuting, because it claims certainty. Hence there must be a certain, immutable, and infallible authority. The only one who can be that authority is God Almighty. All other starting points lack the ability to supply immutability and universals. Christianity is the inescapable truth inasmuch as it alone provides the preconditions for the universal and unchanging laws of logic. Human beings are not omniscient or omnipotent; thus humanity cannot account for the universals in the laws of logic, ethics, and mathematics. Without God, universal and certain claims are unavoidable, and Christianity alone provides the preconditions for universal and certain claims; thus, Christianity must be true.

Without the Triune God, all reasoning fails; thus there could not be science. There is not a non-Christian view of the creation that can make sense out of reasoning, science, and morality. An atheist scientist cannot account for his use of nonphysical logic in his scientific reasoning. Logic is not physical; it is transcendent, universal, and abstract. Only the Christian world and life view can supply the necessary preconditions for the nonmaterial, unchanging, and universal laws of logic. The laws of logic cannot be found in a beaker or a test-tube. You cannot purchase a set of laws of logic on sale at Vons; they are not concrete and physical. Only the transcendent, immutable, universal, and nonphysical God can provide the necessary preconditions for the transcendent, immutable, universal, and nonphysical laws of logic. It is impossible for the atheistic scientist to be correct in declaring that nothing exists except the material. For even that declaration is nonmaterial and hence false. It is impossible for God not to exist.

There Must Be an Absolute Foundation

If one rejects God, one has no absolute, unchanging foundation. A magazine for writers contained an announcement of a new book titled *Composition Number One*. The pages of the book were unnumbered and unbound and could be shuffled randomly like a deck of playing cards. The reader was instructed to arrange the pages haphazardly in any order. "From there the story would unfold," the instructions said. This book is a striking symbol of the unbeliever's worldview. There is no order; it cannot communicate anything meaningful and it contains no logic. Only the Christian worldview provides consistent order and logic. All other worldviews, if they remain within the parameters that their foundation supplies, will be perpetually chaotic, because they cannot supply the needed preconditions for logic and order.

Many skeptics attempt to live a life of order and reason. They have blind faith and believe in the impossible. It is impossible for order to come from chaos and non-life from life. The atheist is in fact a faith-based individual: he has blind faith in the blind process of evolution. I am reminded of Lewis Carroll's *Through the Looking Glass*, which includes the following exchange between Alice and the Queen:

> "I can't believe that!" says Alice.
> "Can't you? Try again, draw a deep breath, and shut your eyes," says the Queen.
> Alice responds, "There's no use trying, one can't believe impossible things."
> "I dare say you haven't had much practice. When I was your

age, I always did it for half an hour a day. Why, sometimes I've believed as many as six impossible things before breakfast."

Those who deny God shut their eyes to God's revelation that is all around them. They cannot kick a can without experiencing God revealing Himself in the beauty and structure of our world, so they wake up every day and believe dozens of impossible things before breakfast. The sun rising, the structure of the house they live in, their families and pets, and breakfast itself all declare that God lives. Order, love, and logic all require the Triune God. Unbelievers cannot argue, think, or live without presupposing the God of scripture. Their worldview is inadequate to explain their experience. Only Christianity can make sense of their experience in this world.

There Is No Reason for Unreason

The non-Christian cannot provide a rational reason why his worldview can account for abstract laws of logic; only the Christian worldview can. The Christian worldview declares that the Triune God is the author of truth and logic. Atheism maintains that laws are relative man-made principals. Such an assumption is self-defeating. The Christian can account for the laws of reason and logic because God is the universal and absolute standard of truth. Thus, the believer can supply the necessary preconditions for the laws of logic because they come from God.

The atheist, however, cannot account for the laws of logic. Logic is universal and the non-Christian cannot provide the required *a priori* conditions for universals. There are no universals in an atheistic worldview. Some atheists assert that the laws of logic are conventions of men; hence, it would be impossible for them to be absolute. But laws by definition must be absolute, or they are not laws at all. Laws are not subject to nose-counting. The laws of logic must be absolute and we must employ them to say anything at all.

If logic is not absolute, then no logical arguments for or against the existence of God could be raised and the atheist would have nothing to work with. Many skeptics tell us that the laws of logic are derived from nature. But this notion does not account for them; it only declares that they exist naturally. One cannot explain logic through science because science depends upon logic to operate; such an explanation would require circular reasoning. The atheist who utilizes logic to try to refute the existence of God has to presuppose His existence while attempting to disprove it. The atheist must assume the absolute laws of logic and borrow from the Christian worldview: The laws of logic can only be explained by the Christian worldview.

Stay True to Scripture

Biblical apologetics takes men's presuppositions seriously. Christians should not compromise and attempt to respond to the unbeliever as though his assumptions about life were as legitimate as Christian assumptions. The anonymous story of the hunter and the bear is applicable:

> As the hunter raised his rifle to shoot the bear, the bear called out, "Can't we talk this over like two sober grown-ups?" The hunter lowered his gun. "What's to talk over?" he asked. "Well, for instance," said the bear, coming closer, "why do you want to shoot me?" "Simple," replied the hunter, "I want a fur coat. It's cold." "All I want is a nice lunch," grinned the bear. "I think we can work this out." So they sat down to work out an agreement. A little while later the bear got up—alone. They had reached a compromise. The bear had received his lunch, and the hunter had on his fur coat.

The truth cannot be compromised. The only possible course of action is to assent to the reality that God alone can provide all the absolute requirements for understanding our world. By rejecting God, one cannot supply the necessary preconditions for logic, morality, and love.

Nothing New Under the Sun

I must note that my approach to defending the faith was not invented by me; it is derived from the work of many scholars and evangelists. In stating this, I am not trying to deflect any criticisms to others. Rather, my goal is to not take credit for the great work of scholars from whom I have learned. My hope is that the following pages will clearly demonstrate that Christianity is certain and true. Only a small part of this book has been conceived by me. I have only fashioned and forged the scholarship of others into a simple way to defend the faith. I will only take blame for any of the philosophical weakness which dwells between the golden nuggets of truth produced by the great men of letters.

Always Be Ready to Give an Answer

"My appeal is to the Word of God," Horatius Bonar, the Scottish theologian and hymnist, writes in *Truth and Error*. "'What are the reasonings, or opinions, or inferences of men? What is the chaff to the wheat?' saith the Lord. Let the Bible decide each question."

Questions about God and about His word are the most important ones we can answer. We are warned in the Bible (2 Timothy 2:23) not to chase down foolish and vain questions—questions such as: Do trees make a noise if they fall in an uninhabited forest? What is the best way to eat corn on the cob: typewriter style or by twirling the cob up and down? What happens to my socks when I put two in the dryer and get only one back? What came first, the chicken or the egg? And why do Wintergreen Life Savers sparkle in the dark when you bite into them? We must disregard the folly of this world's inane curiosity and foolish speculations. We must base our life and worldview on God's infallible revelation; that is where we get the answers to the questions of the ages.

We, like Martin Luther, must stand on the word of God. God's revealed truth is contained within the Bible's pages, and it has all the answers and solutions we will ever need. Vain philosophy—the speculations of bored and deceived men—will never answer any ultimate questions. Spurious New Age doctrines self-destruct under the scrutiny of intelligent questioning. Vain philosophy raises more questions than it can answer. The Bible alone reveals God's will and way for mankind. I have used, and I hope not abused, philosophical insights from the great Christian thinkers. I attempt to tread this ground carefully. Bacon's words are often on my mind: "A little philosophy inclines man's mind to atheism, but depth in philosophy brings men's minds to religion." This book does not attempt to traverse the shadowy forests of the history of philosophy. I believe that all false worldviews can be easily refuted with simple but deep scriptural arguments.

One truth asserted more than any other in this book is that the Christian worldview alone can account for reality and the knowledge of that reality. All other systems of thought cannot account for anything in the world. God's word is the only means to explain all the complexity of the created world. Christianity is not just probably true or hopefully true; it is the only possible foundation for all truth. Only Christianity can provide the necessary preconditions for the intelligibility of human experience. It is impossible for Christianity not to be true, for without it nothing can be known. Reason, ethics, meaning, and any predication can be real and known only if the God of the Bible lives. Christianity is not just known, shown, and demonstrated; the reality is that without the God of scripture, nothing is knowable or intelligible. The necessary precondition for truth, science, value, and personhood is the Triune God of revelation.

Answers Are Possible and Necessary

God has graciously given us His revelation. He has revealed His nature and character to us through scripture. He has given us all the answers we will ever need in His word. The atheist author Ayn Rand was asked by a reporter, "What's wrong with the world?" She replied, "Never before has the world been so desperate for answers to critical questions, and never before has the world been so frantically committed to the idea that no answers are possible." But the believer has the truth and has God-given answers. We have a sure and true confidence that Christ is Lord of all.

The apologetic method I employ comes from Dr. Cornelius Van Til, Dr. Greg Bahnsen, and their numerous disciples. The vocabulary, phrases, and arguments are from their works and not my own. Without their previous scholarship over ninety-percent of this book could not have been written.

The grass withers, the flower fades; but the word of our God stands forever (Isaiah 40:8).

*To Jesus Christ, Savior And Lord, This Book Is Given To My Redeemer,
In Memory Of The Late Greats: Keith Green And Greg Bahnsen,
Diverse, Yet Unified Through The Triune God.*

CHAPTER ONE

WHAT MUST COME FIRST

We have to wonder if atheism resides in the theory or the theorist.[1]

Fundamental propositions, or propositions not deducible from deeper ones, can be established only by showing the complete congruity of all the results reached through the assumption of them.[2]

For three billion years, more or less, the evolution of species proceeded ponderously along a hit-or-miss fashion, until...a sufficiently intelligent species evolved. Then the intelligence took a hand, and evolution was never the same again. The key to evolution is randomness.[3]

Authority and reason have their separate rights: a moment ago one had all the advantage; here the other is queen in her turn.[4]

Francis Schaeffer once pointed out one of the primary problems of our weakened generation: "Our generation is overwhelmingly naturalistic. There is an almost complete commitment to the concept of natural causes in a closed system."[5] Devout atheist Michael Martin, standing on the slumped shoulders of David Hume, brushes off all the classic proofs for the existence of God when he proclaims: "It is difficult to know how, by analogical inference, we arrive [at God]." Martin's laughable book *The Atheist's Handbook* blindly confesses that "It is true that we assume the existence of an explanation for anything we encounter."[7] Yet the Christian, like Madeleine L'Engle, stands on a different platform. "All my false preconceptions get in my way," L'Engle writes, "and these preconceptions surely please Satan, for they turn me from the creator to the tempter who is much more 'reasonable.'"[8] But people are suppressing the truth and they often do this with rational mirages. The Canadian philosopher John Ralston Saul points out that "There is a constant need in our civilization to prefer illusions over reality, a need to deny our perceptions."[9] The presuppositionlist theologian John Heaney makes the following case for reason: "To become a Christian does not mean to renounce reason; on the contrary, it enables a man to become truly rational....[A]t the very heart of [St. Augustine's] thinking is the conviction that the Christian faith alone enables a man to be rational....[A] man must believe in order that he may understand."[10] Therefore Christianity supplies the needed foundation for logic and reason. One cannot reject God and be rationally consistent.

> Now, though Mr. Locke supposes sensation and reflection to be the only two springs of all ideas[,]...abstraction is certainly a different act of the mind.[11]

> It is that knowledge or rudiment of knowledge concerning God, which may be obtained by the contemplation of His creatures; which knowledge may be truly termed divine in respect to the object, and natural in respect to the light. The bounds of that knowledge are, that it sufficeth to convince atheism.[12]

> Explaining and proving that the Christ had to suffer and rise from the dead; this Jesus I am proclaiming to you is the Christ (Acts 17:3).

Apologetics: Defending the Truth of Christianity

Most believers and nonbelievers fail to understand that there can be no neutrality in discussing the way one should look at life. How a man sees the world and interprets reality is determined by the presuppositions he holds. Everyone has presuppositions. All atheists, agnostics, religious people, and Christians have presuppositions. Presuppositions are the lens through which we interpret the world, the basic assumptions we take for granted. These basic assumptions are the preconceived ideas that are rarely challenged; we all have them.

Presuppositions determine what you believe and the way you look at life, and most people are unconscious of them. Nonbelievers have their foundational assumptions about life and the world. They live most of their lives employing basic principles that are inconsistent with their unbelieving worldview. Much of how they live is consistent with the Christian worldview; they take their presuppositions for granted and rarely think about them or follow them to their logical conclusion. All of us should be aware of our assumed biases. We should acknowledge the inclinations that we all bring to the quest for knowledge. We must be tough-minded and answer the question how we know what we know. Steven Schlissel gives us the following amusing illustration regarding presuppositions:

> Presuppositions can function like preferences or tastes, as when you approach a buffet. As you scan the buffet table, without even thinking, you reflexively eliminate what is distasteful to you. You don't even register, say, the pickled carrots. You move on to consider with your eyes only that which your appetite tells you is in the running, and you choose from that. Your preferences and tastes have functioned as a filter, as a presupposition....Yes, your tooshie, like a presupposition, is always with you; it is behind and under everything you do. Yet, you do your lifelong best to keep it hidden and protected. Romans 1:28: "They did not think it worthwhile to retain the knowledge of God." They suppressed God's self-disclosure like passing pickled carrots—neither held any interest for them, being out of sync with their tastes, their presuppositions.[13]

Even the ultra-liberal scholar (and Episcopalian Bishop) John Shelby Spong admitted the reality of rational presuppositions:

> Every human experience is interpreted by the explaining person....It is always interpreted within the framework by which that person comprehends what is real.[14]

We must understand that all thinking people have presuppositions. Islamic fundamentalists have the presupposition that they should imitate the bloodthirsty Muhammad and murder anyone who disagrees with Islam. Evolutionists have the presupposition that life came from non-life and that humanity is nothing more than a souped-up monkey. Atheistic materialists assume that the only thing that exists is the physical universe—no spirits, no angels, no demons, and no God.

Important Definitions

The following definitions are needed to provide clarity in the remainder of the book. If you are not familiar with apologetics and its terminology, you will want to put a bookmark on this page and refer to it until you are fluent with the vocabulary.

- **Apologetics**: The study and application of defending the faith. See 1 Peter 3:15; Jude 3; Acts 17—20.

- *A Priori* **Argument**: An argument prior to or independent of observation and experience, which is assumed to be true without the necessity to prove it. It is fully and universally independent of all experience, discernment, and discovery by the five senses.

- **Empiricism**: The belief that truth is to be found through the use of the five senses. Observation and measurement are the means to discover reality. Truth is discovered by the senses—what we can see, feel, observe, and measure.

- **Epistemology**: The study of how we know what we know, the nature and basis of knowledge, the accounting and justifying of knowledge claims, and the sources and scope of knowledge.

- **Laws of Logic**: Abstract, non-concrete laws of thought and reason that are nonmaterial, universal, obligatory, and absolute. All rational communication and thinking assume the laws of logic. The most well-known law is the law of non-contradiction: A cannot be A and *Not-A* at the same time in the same way. A man cannot be his own father. The laws of logic reflect the nature and mind of God; thus, they have ontological grounding—that is, they are grounded in the very nature of truth itself and cannot be reduced to human convention, opinion, or psychology.

- **Law of Non-Contradiction**: Also known as the Law of Contradiction. A law of logic defined as: "*A* cannot be *A* and *Not-A* at the same time in the same sense." A tall man cannot be a non-man. The law of non-contradiction is an unavoidable and a necessary principle of all rational thought and communication. If the law is denied, then rational thinking is impossible. To deny the law, one must use the law in attempting to deny it. Those who deny the law are participating in a self-refuting effort.

- **Materialism**: The philosophical theory that asserts that only matter exists. There is nothing real beyond the physical world of matter and motion.

- **Naturalism**: A system of thought that asserts that what is ultimately real is only that which belongs to nature and the natural material realm. Matter, energy, and particles in motion are all reality. Nature is all there is.

- **Pragmatism**: The belief that truth is whatever works. If it works best, it is true. Pragmatism asserts that truth is found in the methodologies that work best; it is concerned primarily with what is the most expedient and profitable.

- **Presupposition**: Also known as First Principles. A preeminent belief held to be true and taken as a pre-commitment. It is the belief that is held at the most foundational level of one's grid or web of beliefs. It is the lens through which one interprets reality, taken for granted and assumed in making a statement or a theory. It is one's starting point, primary and fundamental assumption, and metaphysical foundation. Everyone has presuppositions—primary belief patterns that color all one's thought and outlook. Reason, logic, and morality are only consistent with Christian presuppositions.

- **Rationalism**: The belief that truth is found by the right use of reason and logic.

- **Worldview**: An overall perspective of life. One sees and defines the world through his presuppositions. It is the grid that one uses to evaluate reality.

The Standout

Christianity...stands out among all religions...as distinctively "the Apologetic religion."[15]

One of the most important definitions in this book is the definition of the word "presupposition." We all have presuppositions. Bertrand Russell's words in his book *A History of Western Philosophy* are helpful in understanding rational presuppositions: "If you always wore blue spectacles, you could be sure of seeing everything blue." One's presuppositions are the intellectual glasses he wears when he views human experience. An anonymous story tells of the big black spider that declared that it could snag all the flies in Mexico in its new web. After a week had passed and hundreds of flies had been caught in the web, the spider announced that there were no more flies in Mexico. But many of his friends told him they had seen many other flies buzzing around. The prideful spider replied, "They are bees or beetles. They cannot be flies because my web has caught every fly in Mexico. Since my web did not snag them, they cannot be flies." The spider in this story represents the nonbeliever who believes only in what he can see or what he can rationally understand. The web is his mind and his five senses. But God alone is large enough to snag all the flies with His web. He alone can see and understand everything. There is nothing that God cannot know or understand. That is the reason we must use His web as our starting point and lens to look out to the world. Our own webs are too small to understand and account for everything in reality. We must build our worldview on the presupposition that God and His word are the precondition for the intelligibility of our world. Without God's web we cannot account for logic, ethics, science, induction, or even ourselves. Our web is too small, and the world is too large.

Christianity Is the Foundation for Reason

Many non-believing men and women have never made a serious

study of Jesus of Nazareth, yet they spew out of their mouths the assertion that Jesus was just a good moral teacher. These are the words of grandstanding critics. Not only are they criticizing a game which they themselves do not play, but they have not even taken the effort to acquaint themselves with the rules. They are clouds without water, asserting with all personal authority that Christianity is unreasonable, that faith is a blind commitment that attempts to bridge the gap between belief and certainty. As Pascal forcibly stated, "Those who do not love truth excuse themselves on the grounds that it is disputed and that many people deny it."

Some atheists are skilled debaters, like good lawyers with a bad case. Good lawyers can dazzle with clever arguments, and they shout the loudest. They can win the debate although their argument is the weakest. Yet without having Christ and God's word as a metaphysical pre-commitment, the atheist cannot make sense out of anything. He cannot account for the universe, mankind, history, or science. God is the foundation and source of all meaning, purpose, and rationality. God alone makes reason and argument possible. Without God, the unbeliever cannot account for anything in the universe. The Lord is the source of all law, order, logic, mathematics, truth, goodness, beauty, science, and philosophy. The atheist, in reality, has no argument. God must live, or we could not argue at all. I will offer this argument on almost every page of this book; one of my reasons for doing so is that most people do not grasp things the first few times they hear something new. The fictional story of the man who called the operator illustrates this truth. The man dialed Information to get the phone number of *Theater Arts* magazine. "Sorry," said the operator, "there's nobody listed under Theodore Arts." The caller insisted, "It's not a person, it's a publication. I want *Theater Arts*." The operator's voice got testy. "I told you, we have no listing under Theodore Arts." At this point the frustrated caller shouted into the phone: "The word is theater: T-H-E-A-T-E-R." To which the operator responded, "That's no way to spell Theodore." I have taught many people who missed the certainty of the Argument from the Impossibility of the Contrary. So brace yourself for the most powerful apologetic known.

To repeat the basic simple argument: To reason or argue about anything, Christianity must be true. I will be state this argument repeatedly throughout the book; I employ the redundancy so that the reader will never forget that Christianity alone is the precondition of all truth. It is to be hoped that the reader will not get impatient because of this repetition.

Reason and Faith Go Together

Many atheists and skeptics declare that Christianity is opposed to reason. They tell us that faith is unreasonable—simply an illusionary, subjective experience. Freud asserted that people of faith are fearful of reason when it scrutinizes religion. He said, "Where questions of religion are concerned, people are guilty of every possible kind of insincerity and intellectual misdemeanor." I do not doubt that some believers in every generation have been insecure and dishonest about the claims of their religion. But when I have spoken with skeptics, scoffers, atheists, and agnostics, I have found many of them insincere and guilty of intellectual felonies, high crimes, and capital offenses. These intellectual outlaws not only despise the scrutiny of reason and revelation, but generally cower and run when the heat of logic and truth are brought to bear on their worldview. In hundreds of conversations with anti-theists, I have met only a couple dozen who would discuss the truth of worldviews for longer than ten minutes. I have seen hundreds of them snap, snarl, and scream for me to leave when their view of life is challenged. They become quite uncomfortable and want to flee as quickly as possible.

Not only do atheists despise reasoning, they cannot even make reason reasonable. They can be reasonable, but they cannot tell us where reason comes from or why one should be reasonable. They cannot account for or justify human reason. Atheists, when asked why reason is useful, will say, "It just is." Thus, the atheist lives on blind faith. In like manner, the atheist can count, but he cannot account for his counting. He cannot tell you where mathematics comes from; in his view, it just is. There are a great many other things in life that the skeptic takes for granted and cannot justify. He cannot account for his unchanging personhood, for motion, mathematics, morality, or logic.

Non-Christians cannot explain anything. They have no ultimate answers for any part of reality—period. Unbelievers live in a world that they cannot explain.

Jesus: The Logos and Source of Logic

In the beginning was the Word, and the Word was with God, and the Word was God (John 1:1).

Christians are not to be fearful of reason and logic. The apologist R. C. Sproul correctly asserted that "The Christian faith affirms logic not as a law above God but as an aspect built into the Creation which flows from His own character." Jesus is the great logos, and logic is an element of His being and nature. Christians are the only ones who can account for reason; reason comes from the nature of God. The true and living God is a God of reason. Reason cannot be held over His head, but is a reflection of His nature, and we must embrace it in submission to His revelation in the Bible. Christians should base their worldview on God's word and His character. Logic has no physical content. The abstract application of reason also has no material content. Logic is essential and a precondition for any intelligent communication, but was not invented by philosophers. Logic is the foundational instrument necessary for all discourse, debate, science, mathematics, and learning. Without using logic, one could not deny that logic is mandatory for communication. The precondition for the laws of logic is the God of the Bible. Without the sovereign, nonphysical, transcendent, logical, and universal God Almighty, one could not justify or account for transcendent, nonphysical, universal, and abstract logic. God is the precondition for logic. Logic is the precondition for knowledge, discourse, and argument. Logic is absolutely necessary for the intelligibility of life and God is absolutely necessary for logic. Thus God is, and has to be.

Every chapter of this book will emphasize that nonbelievers cannot account for logic or morality. They must use logic, but the laws of logic have no physical form or concrete properties. They are abstract, universal, nonmaterial laws; hence, they do not possess size, weight or shape. They have no biological properties or chemical elements to them. You cannot trip over the laws of logic or pick them up on sale at Wal-Mart. The materialistic atheist cannot give an ultimate grounding or an absolute foundation for the absolute laws of logic. The laws of logic are universal and transcend the material world. Yet there can be nothing transcendent or universal in the atheist's worldview. Atheism is rationally untenable on its own grounds. An atheist cannot argue against Christianity without assuming Christian thought since he depends upon logic to assert his claims. Christianity is logical and true because it rests upon the foundation of the transcendent living God. Only Christianity can provide the necessary precondition for rational thought and logic. We must ground our use of logic on God and His word. He is the final and ultimate universal authority who reigns in sovereign glory. Christian theism is absolutely necessary. It is impossible for it not to be true. It is inescapable.

> In [Christ] are hidden all the treasures of wisdom and knowledge (Colossians 2:3).

The ancient Greek architects held to three standards for building a right building: *Firmitas, utilitas,* and *venustas*; namely, firmness, usefulness, and beauty. God is the only foundation on which we should build a firm, useful, and beautiful worldview. Only Christianity can give us these three traits and more. It provides the foundation by which to justify and utilize all elements of the physical, the abstract, and the spiritual. We might ask: What are the obligatory preconditions for the intelligibility of mankind's experience? What has to be true to make sense out of our world, our experience, and all the various dynamics we take for granted in our day-to-day life? Christianity is the only answer; and even more devastating: Christianity alone can ask the questions and justify them. The unbeliever is left with his mouth stopped up. He must remain silent or admit that he relies on the Christian worldview. God is the precondition for the use of morality, freedom, equality, science, and logic. Without God, one cannot account for reason and the rational use of thought.

When unbelievers use reason, they presuppose and rely on God, even as they are attempting to disprove God. The denial of God presupposes that God lives. Without presupposing the God of the Bible, one cannot rationally assert anything. Remember Van Til's illustration mentioned earlier that the atheist is like the little child on her father's lap who slaps him in the face. In order for her to slap her father, she must sit on his lap. And the atheist, as he attempts to refute the existence of God, must rest on the presupposition that God lives. God must be his presupposition inasmuch as he uses logic and reason to attempt to slap the Lord. Yet as an atheist he cannot account for reason. When he attacks God using logical thought and right reason, he unwittingly borrows from the Christian worldview, which alone can account for reason. So anti-theism presupposes theism. Attacking the existence of God with rational thought actually depends on that which atheists are attempting to disprove. The atheist tries to prove that only the material world is there, all the while using nonmaterial reason. All intellectual warring against the Lord presupposes His existence. We do not have to prove that God exists; everything in the universe shouts His existence.

God Is King; Reason Is His Servant

"Come now; let us reason together," says the LORD (Isaiah 1:18).

The atheist borrows from the Christian worldview when he uses and applies reason. Atheists claim to adore reason and logic. That is why Robert Ingersoll, the nineteenth-century American agnostic, says, "Upon every brain reason should be enthroned as king." Skeptics do not want to bow to God, so they will bow down to an idol, such as human reason. But this way of life creates a problem for them: Without God, they cannot account for reason. A great illustration of this is what happened in the debate between evangelist Ray Comfort and atheist Ron Barrier. Barrier accidentally picked up Comfort's glasses while making his case for atheism. Comfort in his response said to the crowd, "If you are an atheist, you are wearing someone else's glasses." That is what all atheists and unbelievers do: They borrow from the Christian worldview whenever they use reason or morality. Reason and morality are nonmaterial realities that the atheist cannot explain—only the Christian can explain them. Remember: The atheist believes that only the material world exists; to him, reality consists of matter and motion and nothing more. When atheists use and apply logic or morality, they are borrowing Christian glasses. As C. S. Lewis so aptly put it, "I believe in God as I believe that the sun has risen, not because I see it, but because by it I see everything else." The only lens that can make sense of the world and give us vision is God's revealed word.

God Is the Precondition for Knowledge

A man awoke one night at the sound of his car being taken. He ran downstairs. His car was not being stolen; it was being towed. He stopped the driver and asked him why he was taking his car. The driver told him that a movie was being filmed on his street and the director needed the space. The owner of the car asked him how he would have found his car after it had been towed and parked in an unknown location. The driver told him that he would have put a note on the car. That, of course, would not have done the befuddled owner any good, for the car would have been lost, and a note on a lost car is also lost. Such is the problem with the unsaved person. He is lost, and he cannot use his own reason or experience to find his way to truth. He is lost, and his autonomous reason is lost with him. The only way he can find the truth is through an objective, unchanging source. God is that source, and He is immutable.

The Biblical God is the precondition for self-knowledge and the intelligibility of the world. Without God, man is lost holding his own note. Only through God and His revelation can a man be found and have an objective basis for truth. God is the absolute and transcendental necessity for the intelligibility of all human experience. He is the precondition for the grounding and understanding of knowledge. If you do not presuppose the truth of God in Christ, you cannot make sense out of the cosmos and all of reality. Christianity is true not because it makes better sense, but because it alone supplies the foundation for logic; it is true because without it you cannot make sense of anything, anywhere, at any time. All other religions, philosophies, and worldviews lack the transcendentally required precondition for intelligibility, for logic, ethics, and truth.

Jesus said to him, "I am...the truth" (John 14:6).

Every scientist or philosopher who is searching for truth must begin with God and His revelation in Christ. Science is involved with more than rocks, slime, and stars. The concept of truth, beauty, justice, ethics, and reason lie beyond the world of concrete nature. These abstractions cannot be explained in terms of the material world alone. Even the material dynamic within our world cannot be explained in physical terms only. The physical world is made up of organized energy. The materialist cannot explain what energy is or why it "self-organized." The believer can declare God's thoughts after Him, and He has revealed that all power comes from Himself; He organized it for His glory and the delight of mankind. The materialist is always going to be at a loss for words when you ask him for foundational answers; he has none. He cannot account for anything in the physical or nonphysical world.

His worldview is self-defeating, backward, and destructive to science. Whenever he discovers something that will benefit the world, he has breached his worldview, and in that discovery he has borrowed from the Christian worldview. Ultimate and full-fledged materialism contradicts true science and inhibits the motivation for progress.

Empiricism Cannot Supply the Foundation for Knowledge

Many people say that they cannot believe anything unless they can see it for themselves; this is one form of empiricism. Many hold to empiricism as their worldview. They declare that unless something can be tested empirically, using the five senses, it is not true. The main problem with such an assertion is that it cannot itself be tested by any of the senses. Thus it is a self-refuting assertion. Another problem is that our senses are not one-hundred-percent accurate. They are fairly reliable, but cannot be completely trusted. St. Augustine pointed out that a straight oar appears bent when it is in the water. Many of us, as we drive our cars during a hot day, see mirages on the road. If an elephant is a quarter mile up the road and I put my thumb in front of my eyes, the beast seems to be no larger than my thumb. In Las Vegas there are dozens of magicians who make a good living by fooling the empirical senses of their audiences. The hand is quicker than the eye. Our eyes and our other senses can deceive us. We cannot base our world and life view on these senses; nobody can. Skeptics who claim that they only believe in what they see do not and cannot follow that philosophy consistently. Their use of logic, induction, and mathematics is not intelligible by the senses alone; these are nonmaterial entities that the materialist uses every day. To understand this world, God must be presupposed—whether the materialist realizes it or not.

The notion that truth may be ascertained through the senses cannot even justify that two plus two will always be four or that all animals will die. For no one can be simultaneously in all places where two plus two occur, nor can they witness the death of all animals. The believer can trust the basic reliability of the senses only because an infallible God, who knows all things, has told us that we can. The reason scientists often repeat their tests and experiments hundreds of times is because the senses are unreliable. Men of science and industry have built instruments and machines to help bypass the inconsistency and unreliability of the senses.

The five senses are not always reliable because human beings are not infallible and do not have the divine ability to possess universal knowledge. Certain knowledge requires a man to depend on a God who is perfect, infallible, and omniscient. The five senses can provide awareness of and information about only some attributes of an object. Numerous people claim that they only believe what they can see. But in a way, under their non-Christian worldview they cannot see any object. Human eyesight cannot give direct and immediate awareness and understanding of any object. Eyesight can provide information on *some* aspects and attributes of a given object. But only God can see all atoms, and only He can fully understand all protons and electrons. He has exact and exhaustive knowledge of the color, texture, size, weight, density, and complete physical makeup of all objects in the universe. No human can have exhaustive and perfect knowledge of even one of those attributes; yet some want to trust their eyesight and senses above the God who understands all things.

The senses are generally reliable; we know this because of God's revelation in the Bible. We must have a transcendent source that "sees" everything and reveals to us that the senses are basically reliable. The problem comes when people reject God's word and construct a worldview based on their senses alone. Senses can routinely deceive. Professional illusionists get paid large salaries to fool our eyesight. Conversations between husbands and wives can quickly reveal how unreliable the sense of hearing can be. Many taste-test studies have demonstrated that the sense of taste is not always reliable. In 2003, the *Associated Press* reported that surgical teams leave clamps, sponges, and other tools inside 1,500 patients nationwide each year. These are highly trained teams with large potential lawsuits looming over them, and yet their senses fail them at times. One cannot construct a reliable worldview based exclusively on the senses, as many scientists attempt to do. It is impossible for them to avoid the truth of God in view of the fact that all their theories, notes, and scientific conclusions utilize logic. Logic is nonmaterial and invariant and therefore presupposes the God of scripture. Empiricism fails as a worldview every time you stub your toe or trip over a rock. Our senses are normally reliable, but we cannot build a worldview on their reliability. God alone is the precondition for

an intelligible worldview which includes the basic trustworthiness of
our five senses.

Rationalism Cannot Supply the Necessary Preconditions for Knowledge

> According to rationalism, thought is thought of thinking.
> Only that can be known for certain. Once some more specific
> content is specified, certainty disappears. Thus the consistent
> rationalist will deny that there is anything, ultimately, except
> "pure thought," "pure being," etc. Everything else is illusion.
> But what is "pure thought" that is not a thought of something?
> Does that idea have any meaning at all? It is a pure blank.
> The knowledge of which rationalism boasts turns out to be a
> knowledge of...nothing! [17]

Many people declare that they cannot believe anything unless it
is based on reason. They try to make the world intelligible through
rationalism; everything must bow down to human reason. There are
many problems with belief in rationalism. The first problem is the
question: Why? The second problem comes to light when the rationalist
asserts that we should base our lives on rationalism; for when it comes to
ethics, pure rationalism is silent. Still a third problem is that our minds
are as untrustworthy as our empirical senses. Rationalism can discover
the truth about nothing. Our rational capabilities must be built on the
foundation of scripture and the person of God.

Another interesting fact: The mind can conceive and mathematically
prove that perfection exists. Mathematically, one can propose a perfect
circle, a perfect line, and a perfect square. Yet nowhere in our entire
physical universe can one find a perfect line, circle, or square. The
physical universe could not have produced the notion of perfection.
Perfection is based on God's perfect nature. Therefore, in mathematical
theory and geometry, when one studies or discusses perfection, one
presupposes God. God alone is the precondition for perfection; without
God, one could not account for it. How can one fully trust the mind if it
can assert perfection yet no one is able to find perfection in the physical
universe? Ray Comfort addresses this question with an intelligence test
he uses for Christian witnessing.

Take the test quickly. Have someone else read the questions to you and read the question one time only. Do not look over the test before you take it. Record your answers on paper.

1. How many animals did Moses take into the ark?
2. What is the name of the RAISED PRINT that deaf people use?
3. Is it possible to end a sentence with the word "the"?
4. Spell the word "shop." What do you do when you come to a green light?
5. It is noon. You look at the clock. The big hand is on the three. The little hand is on the five. What time is it?
6. Spell the word "silk." What do cows drink?
7. Listen carefully: you are the driver of a train with thirty people on board. At the first stop ten people get off. At the next stop, five people get on. What is the name of the train driver?[18]

The answers may be found at the end of this chapter. Most people get the majority of the questions wrong. The questions are actually really simple, but our minds cannot always be trusted; they are not perfectly dependable. We cannot make sense out of the world using reason alone. We must rely on God, who alone is the precondition to make sense out of our world. He, exclusively, is perfect and infallible. The world is real, and our real human minds can know its nature because God has given us our minds and has revealed to mankind that the world can be known. Our minds are not infallible, and that is one of the major problems with rationalism. There is no reason to trust man's autonomous reason.

Modernity Hates Conversion

The notion that Christ is the only way to God is not tolerated in our secular culture. Secularism declares that conservative Christianity will strap an intellectual straitjacket on society—a bondage that will infringe on the personal rights and liberties of "free" individuals. The action of converting one to Christ is thought to be arrogant and egotistical. But Jesus Christ is the only way to God. Who else died for you and supplies the necessary precondition for logic and morality? John Stott makes the case this way: "To cultivate a mind so broad that it can accommodate every opinion, however false or evil, without ever detecting anything to reject, is not a virtue; it is the vice of the feeble minded and amoral." The teachings of Jesus are clearly and radically intolerant. Jesus is the only way. He is *the* truth.

The Lover of Wisdom

God's word reveals the only true philosophy. All other schools of thought are vain, and we must cast down vain imaginations and take all thoughts captive. In the Bible Paul instructs us not to embrace the vain philosophy of non-Christian thought. Scores of people in the modern church falsely believe that Paul disannuls all philosophy. But the imperative is against a particular type of philosophy; vain philosophy is what God disallows. All philosophy not based on God's revelation is empty, barren, and vain, and the Bible prohibits it. Philosophy derived from Biblical revelation, however, can expose bad arguments and bring forth light through good arguments.

Therefore he reasoned in the synagogue with the Jews and with the Gentile worshipers, and in the marketplace daily (Acts 17:17).

Men are never to attempt to put God on trial. There is no external standard that can judge God or His word. Historical, archeological, mathematical, and other evidences are not to judge the Bible's truthfulness as the word of God. A man cannot certify or rubber-stamp the Bible as a revelation from God. It is impossible for the Bible not to be the word of God. God must be true for anything in this life to be intelligible. God is the requirement for evidences and the law of non-contradiction. No external authority is to be used to verify the Bible as a revelation from God. Mankind cannot be the authority; evidences cannot be the authority: Only the Lord can be the ultimate authority. To make sense of this world, we must start with God and His revealed word. There is nothing that we can use independently of God's authority. The laws of logic, historical evidences, archeological finds, tests, and experiments all presuppose the Triune God. We do not need to verify or test God's word; it has authority, and without it, we cannot make sense of any element or concept in the world. God is, and He does not need to be justified. Lost mankind alone needs justification.

Proof and More Proof, Nothing But Proof

It is an eye-opening experience to watch evolutionists scramble around trying to get "evolutionary warning stickers" off textbooks and intelligent design curricula out of the public schools. What are they afraid of? Maybe the evidence: Such as the Tyrannosaurus Rex that was found with its blood vessels intact and still flexible after almost 70 million years. It would not just be implausible but impossible for soft tissue and blood to be intact that long. Even ten thousand years would seem impossible. This is one reason the evolutionists are running scared. And yes, the Bible reveals to humanity that the earth hangs on nothing (Job 26:7) and is a sphere (Isaiah 40:22). Scripture declared these facts thousands of years before telescopes and modern science discovered them. God's word instructs His people how to wash their hands to ward off infections and disease (Leviticus 15:13). God's word declared to humanity the proper function of the water cycle (Job 38:12-14), the existence of ocean currents (Psalms 8:8), the solar cycle, and the expansion of the universe (Isaiah 40:22) centuries before modern science discovered these truths. These facts are consistent with the authority of the Bible. They, and other evidence, do not give the Bible authority; it is endued with it because it is God's word, and all science, testing, and examination presuppose biblical revelation. Testing utilizes a number of disciplines, such as logic and induction. A materialistic worldview cannot justify the existence or the use of the laws of reason; they are nonphysical and abstract laws that can only come from the nature of the one true and living God. We have sure knowledge that the God of scripture lives. We do not think He *probably* exists; our faith is not just *reasonable* or *plausible*. It is impossible for the true and living God *not* to exist, because without Him we can know nothing at all. He is the precondition for all knowledge. God must be presupposed as the basis of every element of mankind's experience, knowledge, and value.

God Is the Foundation of All Reality

Consider the following syllogism:

1. The God of scripture is the foundation of all reality or reality is unintelligible.

2. Reality is intelligible.

3. Therefore, God is the foundation of reality.

The consequence of asserting that God does not exist is that the world becomes unintelligible and unknowable. But the proposition is impossible because it is self-refuting. If the world is unintelligible and unknowable, then that statement itself would be unintelligible and unknowable, hence self-voiding and false. Consequently, God must be the ground and foundation of knowledge. Unless Christianity is true, we can know nothing of reality. If we can know nothing of reality, we cannot know even the proposition that we do not know. Unless the God of revelation is and has spoken, human knowledge has no intelligible basis. Harry Blaimires points out that "No one can pretend [the Old and the New Testament are not] there. Everyone who is concerned with the meaning of life and the destiny of the human race will have to take [them] into account."[19] God's word declares that life must revolve around Him. We must have no other gods before Him. All men have a destiny that will find its consummation at the judgment seat of Christ. Self-deceivers can pretend that God does not exist, but God lives. Those who pretend He has not spoken live a contradictory and confusing life. Their life will end one day and they will give an account for it. This truth must constantly remain in front of our eyes. We should live and move before the face of God; that is our duty and our joy.

There are many professional skeptics and scoffers in our culture who marshal their full-blown nastiness to defend atheism. These men attempt to act sagacious as they employ their acerbic wit to attack God. They become experts at wishful thinking and self-deception. They have elaborate arguments that instruct the blind how to stay in the dark while professedly becoming wise.

An Anti-theist

Combative atheist Michael Martin pontificates that "belief in the incarnation is clearly unjustified. Not only is the evidence for the incarnation lacking, but it is incoherent and conceptually problematic."[20] This statement, denying the reality of the non-material, lacks evidence and is more than problematic. Martin cannot even account for the reality of evidence or the discovery of apparent problems. He must stand on the Christian worldview to discuss evidence and problems.

Only Christianity can have a justified basis for the evaluation of evidence and the intelligent identification of problems. Martin's "case" is unintelligible because his assertion disqualifies itself. Thus his atheism is self-defeating, like all systems that reject God's word. Atheism proclaims materialism—the belief that all reality is composed only of physical material. Yet the assertion of materialism is not itself made up of anything material. The atheist's view cannot support or justify itself. Atheism is a non-material system that teaches that the non-material does not exist. Thus it pops its own philosophical balloon. Proposing any philosophy, including that only the material world exists, is a non-material exercise. When one propagates anything, he is affirming through his use of non-material assertions and critiques that God lives. By claiming to be a materialist, one is actually assenting to anti-materialism.

God Completes All That He Begins

> Thus says the LORD, the King of Israel, and his Redeemer, the LORD of hosts: "I am the First and I am the Last; beside Me, there is no God. And who can proclaim as I do? Then let him declare it and set it in order for Me....Let them show these to them. Do not fear, nor be afraid; have I not told you from that time, and declared it? You are My witnesses. Is there a God besides Me? I have declared the former things from the beginning; They went forth from My mouth, and I caused them to hear it. Suddenly I did them, and they came to pass.... Even from the beginning I have declared it to you; before it came to pass I proclaimed it to you....You have heard; see all this. And will you not declare it?...Come near to Me, hear this: I have not spoken in secret from the beginning; from the time that it was, I was there. And now the Lord GOD and His Spirit have sent Me. Thus says the LORD, your Redeemer, The Holy One of Israel: I am the LORD your God" (Isaiah 44:6-8; 48:3-20).

Another area of proof is the Messianic prophecies fulfilled by Jesus Christ. The Tenach (Old Testament) foretold the coming of the Messiah in exact detail. The text, written centuries before the coming of Jesus, prophesied over three hundred facts about Him. No other founder of any religion can provide a similar record of his life written centuries before his birth. Religious founders like Joseph Smith, Mary Baker Eddy, David Koresh, Muhammad, and Buddha cannot supply a widely transmitted, preexisting record that accurately prophesied the details of their lives. The three hundred clear prophecies of the coming Messiah were ordained by God. The Lord revealed historical facts about the coming of Jesus prior to His birth. All these prophecies came to pass in the birth, life, death, and resurrection of Jesus of Nazareth.

Christ's virgin birth was foretold about seven hundred years before He was born: "So, the Lord Himself shall give you a sign. Behold, the virgin will conceive and shall bring forth a son, and they shall call His name Emmanuel" (Isaiah 7:14). His place of birth was foretold: "And you, Bethlehem...out of you He shall come forth to Me, to become Ruler in Israel, He whose goings forth have been...from eternity" (Micah 5:2). The exact date of His entry in Jerusalem was foretold in the book of Daniel. God revealed the coming of Palm Sunday: "Rejoice greatly, O daughter of Zion! Shout, O daughter of Jerusalem! Behold, your King is coming to you; He is just and having salvation, lowly and riding on a donkey, a colt, the foal of a donkey" (Zechariah 9:9).

Christ's death on the cross was foretold before that form of execution was even invented. Psalms 22:1-16 announced the crucifixion hundreds of years before it happened: "I am a worm, and no man; a reproach of men, and despised by the people. All who see me laugh me to scorn; they shoot out the lip; they shake the head, saying, He trusted on the LORD; let Him deliver him; let Him rescue him, since He delights in him!...I am poured out like water, and all my bones are spread apart; my heart is like wax; it is melted in the midst of my bowels and you have brought me into the dust of death. For dogs have circled around me; the band of spoilers have hemmed me in, they pierced my hands and my feet." This evidence is overwhelming. The truth is even more certain and compelling than great blocks of evidence one might compile to prove the facts of Christianity. The argument for Jesus Christ is certain. Without God, one cannot provide the necessary preconditions for truth and certainty.

The Triune God Exists: The Certain Argument

God is in heaven; He does whatever He pleases (Psalms 115:3).

The simple Biblical argument is: Without God one cannot account for anything. God is the precondition for logic, morality, mathematics, and everything else in the cosmos. This truth will be continuously hammered throughout this book, so that when you are finished, you will know it inside and out. The truth is simple and powerful; to understand it, most of us must hear the argument echo and re-echo.

One must be certain of something, because to assert that no one can know anything for certain would require one to be certain of at least that. There has to be certainty in our world to know anything. And we must know something, or again we fall into self-refutation. The problem is that, to know anything, one must either have all knowledge or hear from one who does. Only an omniscient being can know universals and absolutes. No finite man could know universals unless an omniscient and infinite being revealed it to him. And God has revealed truth and logic to man; therefore, we can have knowledge. Without God one can have no knowledge; a self-refuting proposition. Thus it is certain that God must live.

As a young man, Mark Twain took a job as a newspaper reporter. He was instructed by his editor never to state anything as a fact that he could not verify himself from personal knowledge alone. His first assignment was to cover a social event. After the event, Twain turned in the following story:

> A woman, *representing* her name to be Mrs. James Jones, is *reported* to be one of the city's leading society figures. It is *said* that today she gave what *purported* to be a party for a number of *alleged* ladies. The hostess *claims* to be the wife of a man *reputed* to be a local physician.

Twain demonstrated that we must have prior rational commitments to make any claim. There must be many things we presuppose in order to communicate with others. All those necessary presuppositions make dialogue possible. Thus without presupposing the existence of God, one could not account for communication. Language and communication would be impossible without God. But we do communicate, and we would have to communicate even to deny God.

The great thing about the "argument from the impossibility of the contrary" is that it grows in power when the unbeliever attacks it. The argument grows in force because the unbeliever must use logic to make an intellectual challenge. Yet logic requires God. Only Christianity supplies the necessary preconditions for logic. Thus every time an unbeliever rationally attacks God he is demonstrating that God lives. Without God, no rational assertion could be made. Every time a person says anything, he is increasing the force of the argument that God lives. The old 1950's science-fiction movie *The Blob* illustrates this point. The blob grows larger and stronger every time someone uses a weapon in attempting to kill it. The blob is ready to take over America, and the President orders the army to hit it with an atomic bomb. The troops launch the bomb, and as the mushroom cloud slowly starts to dissipate and the smoke clears, they are stunned by the horror of horrors—the blob has survived. Not only has the blob survived, it now is ten times larger. The blob absorbed the massive energy from the bomb and did not get weaker but grew in size and strength. Similarly, unbelievers will attempt to fire intellectual weapons at the "argument from the impossibility of the contrary." Nevertheless, all their attacks will only be consumed by the truth, while the defense of the truth grows stronger and larger. There is nothing a skeptic can assert without ultimately relying on theism, since God alone provides the preconditions for the laws of logic. Thus the unbeliever's argument will always presuppose God because the unbeliever cannot himself supply the preconditions for the nonmaterial laws of logic.

The Triune God is the preexisting foundation for all debate. Deny God and one cannot debate anything. Even Kant, like a man awakened at night from a deep slumber, stumbled on to something when he wrote, "I think to myself merely the relation of a being, in itself completely unknown to me, to the greatest possible systematic unity of the universe." The start of this assertion is self-refuting. He has a relation to a being—God—that is "completely unknown" to himself; of course he does know at least that about this being. Thus he refutes his notion that he does not know anything about God. Kant staggers in his tired state and falls to the floor in his agnosticism. Kant was right when he stated that God brings about the "greatest possible unity in the universe." Only the truth of God can supply the foundation for employing logic and our empirical senses. God alone unifies all the diversity in the universe and all its particulars.

God has raised up [Christ], having loosed the pains of death,

because it was not possible that He should be held by it....
Therefore let all the house of Israel know assuredly that God
has made this same Jesus, whom you crucified, both Lord and
Christ (Acts 2:24 & 36).

Answers to the Test

1. None. Noah was on the ark, not Moses.
2. Deaf people do not use raised print.
3. The question is an example of one.
4. Go.
5. Noon.
6. Water.
7. You are the driver of the train.

Notes

[1] John P. Koster, Jr., *The Atheist Syndrome* (Brentwood, TN: Wolgemuth
& Hyatt, 1989), p. 25.

[2] Herbert Spencer, *First Principles* (New York: D. Appleton, 1900), p.
495.

[3] Isaac Asimov, *Science Past — Science Future* (New York: Ace Books, 1975),
p. 207.

[4] Blaise Pascal, *Concerning the Vacuum* (Chicago: University of Chicago,
1982), p. 357.

[5] Francis Schaeffer, *True Spirituality* (Wheaton, IL: Tyndale House, 1971),
p. 60.

[6] Michael Martin, *Atheism: A Philosophical Justification* (Philadelphia:
Temple University Press, 1990), p. 130.

[7] B. C. Johnson, *The Atheist Debater's Handbook* (Amherst, NY: Prometheus
Books, 1981), p. 61.

[8] Madeleine L'Engle, *The Genesis Trilogy* (Colorado Springs: Waterbrook Press, 1997), p. 30.

[9] John Ralston Saul, *Voltaire's Bastards: The Dictatorship of Reason in the West* (New York: Random House, 1992), p. 11.

[10] John Heaney, *Faith, Reason, and the Gospels* (Westminster, MD: Newman), pp. 80-81.

[11] Isaac Watts, *Logic* (Morgan, PA: Soli Deo Gloria Publications, First Printed 1724; Reprinted 1996), p. 81.

[12] Francis Bacon, *The Advancement of Learning* (London: Dent & Sons, 1957), p. 88.

[13] Steve M. Schlissel, *The Revisionists' Tooshies* (Vallecito, CA: Chalcedon Report, September 2000), p. 23.

[14] John Shelby Spong, *Rescuing the Bible from Fundamentalism* (San Francisco: Harper Collins, 1991), p. 25.

[15] B. B. Warfield, *Selected Shorter Writings of B.B. Warfield II* (Nutley, NJ: P & R, 1973), pp. 99-100.

[16] R. C. Sproul, John Gerstner, & Arthur Lindsey, *Classical Apologetics* (Grand Rapids: Zondervan, 1984), p. 76.

[17] John Frame, *The Doctrine of the Knowledge of God* (Phillipsburg, NJ: P & R, 1987), p. 61.

[18] Ray Comfort, *The Ten Commandments* (Bellflower, CA: Living Waters, 1993), p. 192.

[19] Harry Blaimires, *On Christian Truth* (Ann Arbor, MI: Servant Books, 1983), p. 129.

[20] Michael Martin, *The Case Against Christianity* (Philadelphia, PA, 1991), p. 156.

CHAPTER TWO

CHRISTIANITY HAS ALL THE EVIDENCE

Any logical argument against the existence of God affirms the existence of God. All atheists and agnostics assume the laws of logic, but cannot account for them. A physical world cannot produce nonphysical laws of logic. If there is such a thing as proof then there is logic, thus, there is a God.[1]

Christianity...stands out among religions...as distinctively the Apologetic religion.[2]

Christian philosopher Colin Brown gives this wise definition of faith: "A Faith which goes on believing despite the evidence is not a faith worth having. The Biblical idea of faith is trust in God because of what God has said and done."[3] Many people in our culture do not understand this idea. Aggressive anti-theist Richard Dawkins gives a different definition of faith: "Faith is the great cop-out, the great excuse to evade the need to think and evaluate evidence. Faith is belief despite, even perhaps because of, the lack of evidence.[4] The Bible asserts a partnership of faith and reason: "He also presented Himself alive after His suffering by many infallible proofs, being seen by them during forty days and speaking of the things pertaining to the kingdom of God" (Acts 1:3).

The Overwhelming Evidence for God in Christ

Present your case, says the LORD; bring forth your strong reasons, says the King of Jacob. Let them bring forth and show us what will happen; let them show the former things,

what they were, that we may consider them, and know the
latter end of them; or declare to us things to come. Show the
things that are to come hereafter, that we may know that you
are gods; yes, do good or do evil, that we may be dismayed, and
see it together (Isaiah 41:21-23).

There is overwhelming evidence that God exists, but the evidence
alone will not convert a skeptic into a saint. The bare facts of the
more than three hundred Messianic prophecies are astounding and
convincing to me as a Christian. I love the evidence that God has given
us. The prophecies that foretell the birth, life, and death of Jesus are
found in Genesis 3:15, 49:10; Psalms 2:6-7; Psalms 22, Micah 5:2; Daniel
9:25; Zechariah 9:9, 12:10; Isaiah 7:14, 9:6, 53; and many other passages.
These prophecies, as recorded in the Dead Sea Scrolls and the ancient
Jewish Targums (translations of the Old Testament into Aramaic), were
written before the birth of Christ; and every one of them was fulfilled
by Jesus.

Apologist Peter Stoner, a former professor of science, calculated
the odds as 10^{157} that merely forty-eight of these predictions could be
fulfilled by chance. The Theory of Probability declares that odds greater
than 10^{50} are the same as zero; and 10^{157} is much larger than that. Hence
the life of Jesus was ordained by God Almighty. There are many self-
styled prophets active in our world today. The tabloids have prophecies
and predictions that they share with the world (for a fee). In the 1990's
the *National Enquirer* predicted fifty-five occurrences; none came true.
The Messianic prophecies are different and unique. The accuracy and
specific detail of the events that the Bible prophesied are astonishing.
They are not vague generalities; the Messianic prophecies are bold,
startling, detailed, and specific.

All things must be fulfilled, which were written in the Law
of Moses, the Prophets, and the Psalms concerning Me (Luke
24:44).

The historical and Biblical testimony concerning the resurrection
of Christ is convincing to me and other believers as well. Those outside
the true faith have a different set of presuppositions which complicates
the communication of the evidence. The scriptures do not instruct us
to press the *prima facie* evidence, but to profess the *A Priori* necessity
of the truth of Christianity. God does not *probably* exist. The argument
from the impossibility of the contrary demonstrates that God *must*

exist. God is the precondition for all argument, proof, evidence, and reason. It is impossible for God not to exist, inasmuch as He is the precondition for all intelligent exchanges. The nonphysical, universal, and unchanging God alone provides the necessary preconditions for the use of nonphysical, universal, invariant laws of logic. To argue at all, one must presuppose that God lives. It is impossible for Jesus not to be Lord of all.

The truth of God's existence is not probable; it is certain. God's existence is the absolute precondition for all our questions and doubts. We utilize logic in our questions as well as in our doubts, thereby affirming that God lives. Christianity is the only worldview that provides human reason a foundation for its proper function. Non-Christian systems of thought cannot furnish a foundation for the law of non-contradiction; thus, those systems of thought can only offer self-contradictory worldviews. Unless one believes in the Triune God, one cannot account for human experience. God is the precondition for all argument, proof, evidence, and reason. All human thought requires the employment and assumption of the universal and invariant laws of logic. Only the transcendent, nonphysical, and unchanging holy God provides the necessary preconditions for the use of nonphysical, universal, and unchanging laws of logic. To argue at all, one must presuppose that the true and living God exists.

The Questions

The opposite of Christianity is impossible inasmuch as all other worldviews fall into absurdity, self-contradiction, and conclusions contradictory to their own assumptions. An important part of life is to ask questions. The primary question one must ask is: What will supply the preconditions to make reality intelligible? Without God, nothing comports with reality and nothing can make sense; that is the Biblical truth. The true and living God is the precondition for the intelligibility of reality and the understanding of all human experiences. The truth from the word of God will dislodge unbelievers from their self-deceptions and delusions because of the self-defeating nature of their intellectual pre-commitments.

Evidence Is Wonderful

Evidence is indeed wonderful. The Christian faith has a lot of evidence to support its claims. In truth, there is nothing *but* evidence for the God of the Bible. Every star and every atom declares the majesty of God (Psalm 19:1). We see the evidence of God's fingerprints in every corner of the universe. Mankind discovers the proof and affirms the facts that the Bible records and announces. The greatest miracle is the resurrection of Jesus. Jesus Christ is alive! He is the only religious leader in history to rise from the dead. He is the only one who promised a resurrection, and He kept His promise. You can visit the tombs of all the deceased religious leaders and find their remains still in the grave. The great-grandson of Mahatma Gandhi, in the late 1990's, took Gandhi's ashes to the Ganges River as thousands of onlookers sang and chanted. He opened the copper urn and dropped Gandhi's ashes in the river, proving that Gandhi was still dead. Recently in Israel, the Muslims and the Jewish people have fought for control of the tomb of Abraham, Isaac, and Jacob. You can visit their occupied graves just as you can those of heterodox leaders like Mary Baker Eddy, Joseph Smith, and Muhammad. They and all the others died and stayed dead; their occupied tombs attest to it. Jesus, however, is alive. His grave is empty.

Jesus said, "All power on earth and heaven has been given to me" (Matthew 28:18). No force could have kept Him down. The Romans killed Him, put Him in a cave tomb, and placed huge boulder at a downward angle in front of the cave, pasted Caesar's seal on the crypt, and posted Roman guards to protect the tomb. They were only trying to prevent the inevitable. Jesus had the power to rise, and nobody could stop Him. God used Christ's resurrection and appearance before His disciples, and He used the subsequent preaching of the Apostles, to win many of Christ's enemies to salvation. The Bible tells us that "the word of God spread, and the number of the disciples multiplied greatly in Jerusalem; and a great many of the priests were obedient to the faith" (Acts 6:7). Scripture also records that some Pharisees converted to Christianity (Acts 15:5).

Men do not die willingly if they know they have been deceived. The followers of Jim Jones — the people who knew that he was a fraud — tried to escape Jonestown. Once they knew that Jones was an impostor and had whipped up a batch of poisoned Kool-Aid, they ran and hid in the jungle. Many others tried to escape and were shot. They knew Jones was a charlatan and did not want to die for him. However, the Apostles and hundreds of others in the first century did die for Jesus, because they knew He was risen.

The first-century followers of Christ died knowing that He was sinless. Many followers spent day and night with Him for over three years; they knew He was sinless. If you spent sixty minutes with any other human, you would soon find out that he was not perfect. You would not lay down your life declaring that he was sinless. You would not die for what you knew was a lie. David Koresh understood this problem, since he was a cunning deceiver. Knowing that his followers would observe him sinning every day, he devised a crafty way to avoid the problem of a sinner claiming to be the Messiah. Koresh called himself the "sinful Messiah." The antithesis to Koresh is Jesus; Christ's friends and enemies all confessed that He had never sinned. The disciples, including His betrayer, Judas; His religious enemies; and His Roman enemies were all in agreement on one subject: Jesus never sinned. No one could accuse Jesus of sin. Jesus is alive as the sinless Messiah; that is a fact. It is not a brute fact that stands by itself and awaits the judgment of man, but it is true, and it is impossible for it not to be true.

Love Presupposes God

Love suffers long, and is kind; love does not envy; love does not parade itself, is not puffed up; does not behave rudely, does not seek its own, is not provoked, thinks no evil; does not rejoice in iniquity, but rejoices in the truth; bears all things, believes all things, hopes all things, endures all things. Love never fails (1 Corinthians 13:4-8).

God is love (1 John 4:8).

As you study these pages, one thing will become clear: The skeptic and the nonbeliever cannot account for or justify anything. They cannot tell the informed believer, under the scrutiny of truthful investigation, where anything comes from or why one should affirm any notion. Only the Christian worldview can account for logic, ethics, identity, motion, induction, and even love. Ask the atheist, "What is love? Is it a pat on the head, or a hug and a kiss for one's wife?" No. A man can hate his wife and still give her a hug and a kiss. Love is more than a touch or an agitating flux of hormones and neurotransmitters in the brain. Love is grounded in the nature of God. The one and true God is the Father, Son, and Holy Spirit. Throughout eternity, the heavenly Father loved the Son and the Holy Spirit. The Spirit loved the Father and the Son, as the Son also loved the Father and the Spirit. Only the one eternal God in three persons can tell us where love came from and what love is. No other religion can justify or ultimately explain love, because their gods do not coexist in one being as infinite, immutable, and loving persons. The Father, Son, and Holy Spirit have eternal, unchanging love among the Godhead. Yahweh alone is God, and He alone can be the eternal ground for love. The love and the fellowship among the persons in the Godhead are the pattern and the source of human love and interpersonal communication. We love others because we bear the image of God. There are three persons in the Godhead—the Father, the Son, and the Holy Spirit—and these three are one God, the same in substance, equal in power and glory.

Only Christianity Can Account for Love

If you reject Christianity, let me ask you some questions: Where did love come from and what is love? Is love just a physical action? If a woman pinches the cheeks of her grandchild and kisses her husband when he goes to work, is that love? No. A woman could do that, all the while plotting to murder them. The non-Christian cannot give an answer that is grounded in unchanging truth. The nonbeliever will not have any ultimate answers. Asking questions is one of the best tools to force people out of self-deception and atheism. The nonbeliever cannot even account for questioning; but the Christian can. The skeptic has no ultimate answers. Only Christianity can account for love. Love comes to us through the Triune God. God's nature is the ultimate and objective basis of love. Real love is objective and eternal because it is an eternal attribute of the eternal God. God presupposes love, and love presupposes God. Christians can justify love, and we should share that love.

The God of the Bible Is the Only True and Living God

You are My witnesses, says the LORD, and My servant whom I have chosen; that you may know and believe Me, and understand that I am He. Before Me there was no God formed, nor shall there be after Me. I, even I, am the LORD, and besides Me there is no savior (Isaiah 43:10,11).

The only true God is the Father, the Son, and the Holy Spirit: one God in three persons. There is no other God in whom we must believe. He is the only God who lives and the only God who is necessary.

Excuses and Iniquity

For the iniquity of his covetousness I was angry and struck him; I hid and was angry, and he went on backsliding in the way of his heart (Isaiah 57:17).

Most of the questions that unbelievers ask are not sincere inquiries but excuses to justify a sinful lifestyle. Anyone can be a skeptic and ask fatuous questions. There is a story in the Talmud in which one Rabbi rules on the ownership of a wild bird. Rabbi Eliezer serves as the community's judge and He adjudicates this dispute. He says, "If the bird is found within fifty cubits of a man's land, the bird is his property. If it is found outside the fifty cubits, it belongs to the person who discovers it." After this ruling, Rabbi Jeremiah attempts to stultify Eliezer with the question, "If one foot of the bird is discovered in the limit of the fifty cubits and another foot is on the other side, outside the fifty cubits, what is the law?" The Talmud goes on to say, "It was for that question that Rabbi Jeremiah was thrown out of the house of study."

People can ask an endless number of questions, and frequently they do not really want the answers. It is easy to ask imprudent questions and be a dime-store skeptic. It is a lot more challenging to be tough-minded. Most of the world does not like to evaluate its own worldview and ask the difficult questions. The tenacity of unbelievers' self-deception is extraordinary. They suppress the truth with herculean strength in view of the fact that they know God exists, but they do not want to be intellectually honest. Error begets error, and deception begets deception. The more they suppress the truth, the more they embrace lies and inconsistencies. They are quick to adapt strange esoteric beliefs and practices in an attempt to fortify their disbelief in God.

It is comforting to know not only that there is incredible evidence for Christianity, but that everything in existence is evidence for God. In St. Thomas Aquinas's words, "I see His face in every flower." It is not so much that we have to prove theism, but we are called to realize that all proof presupposes the God of the Bible.

The nonbeliever will make many claims that contradict his own worldview—claims about universal truths, absolute morality, the laws of logic, and so on. But universal claims of knowledge are inconsistent with an atheistic worldview, because atheism fails to provide a basis for such claims. The great thing about the presuppositional apologetic of Cornelius Van Til is that it can refute all non-Christian worldviews and is incredibly powerful because it is derived from the Bible. Christianity is the only worldview that supplies human reason with a basis for its proper function. No non-Christian system of thought can furnish a foundation for the law of non-contradiction; thus, those systems of thought can only offer a self-contradictory worldview.

Unless you believe in God's revealed word, you can consistently and logically believe in nothing else. God is the precondition for all argument, proof, evidence, and reason. It is impossible for God not to exist. He is the precondition for all intelligent communication, since communication requires one to use the laws of logic. Only the nonmaterial, universal, and unchanging God can provide the necessary preconditions for the use of nonmaterial, universal, and unchanging laws of logic. To argue at all, one must presuppose that God lives. Non-believing thought cannot supply the necessary prior foundation for the laws of logic, hence results in futility because of the internal contradictions in which it is entangled. Thus the contrary of Christianity is impossible since it falls into absurdity and is self-contradictory. All non-Christian worldviews lead to conclusions that are incongruous with their premises. The primary question we should ask is: What will supply the preconditions that make reality intelligible? The reality is that without God, nothing can make sense. The true and living God is the source and absolute basis for the intelligibility of reality and the understanding of all human experiences.

Notes

[1] Greg Bahnsen, *Bahnsen and Gordon Stein Debate 1985* (Irvine, CA: Covenant Media, 1985). [Cassette tape recording.]

[2] B. B. Warfield, *Selected Writings of B. B. Warfield II* (Nutley, NJ: P & R, 1973), pp. 99-100.

[3] Colin Brown, *Philosophy and the Christian Faith* (Downers Grove, IL: Intervarsity Press, 1968), p. 284.

[4] Richard Dawkins, *Servant Magazine* (Winter 2000), p. 8.

CHAPTER THREE
ATHEISTS MUST GUARD THEIR
FAITH CAREFULLY

If a man walked down the railway track, saw a train racing toward him, closed his eyes, and said, "I believe it's a marshmallow train," would it change reality? What he believes doesn't matter. What matters is that if he doesn't get off the track, he will be a marshmallow.[1]

A young Atheist cannot guard his faith too carefully. Dangers lie in wait for him on every side.[2]

Atheism is too simple. If the whole universe has no meaning, we should never have found out that it has no meaning.[3]

C. S. Lewis, when he was an atheist, was very rankled at God. He admitted it this way: "I was at this time living, like so many atheists or anti-theists, in a whirl of contradictions. I maintained that God did not exist. I was also very angry with God for not existing. I was equally angry with Him for creating the world."[4] Bahnsen nailed the problem on the head: "The conception of God is necessary for the intelligible interpretation of any fact."[5] Even the skeptic David Hume confessed: "Solidity...is perfectly incomprehensible alone....Our modern philosophy, therefore, leaves us no just nor satisfactory idea of solidity; nor consequently of matter."[6] Matter alone cannot supply the necessary prior conditions for nonmaterial dynamics such as logic and morality.

For the wrath of God is revealed from heaven against all ungodliness and unrighteousness of men, who suppress the truth in unrighteousness, because what may be known of God is manifest in them, for God has shown it to them. For since the creation of the world His invisible attributes are clearly seen, being understood by the things that are made, even His eternal power and Godhead, so that they are without excuse, because, although they knew God, they did not glorify Him as God nor were thankful, but became futile in their thoughts, and their foolish hearts were darkened. Professing to be wise, they became fools (Romans 1:18-22).

Hearts Lost in Deception and Despair

Madalyn Murray O'Hair, on the night of her consecration to the faith of atheism, shook her fists at the sky and declared to heaven, "I do not believe in you." If God did not exist, at whom was she shaking her fist? I love the story of the famous nineteenth-century skeptic Robert Ingersoll, who delivered a speech that attempted to prove that God did not exist. He rambled on and on with reasons why he did not believe in God. At the end of the lecture he challenged God to strike him dead if He exists. Nothing happened, and Ingersoll left with great satisfaction. After he left, an atheist asked a Christian, "Didn't Ingersoll prove something tonight?" Her reply was memorable. "Yes, he did," she answered. "He proved that God isn't taking orders from an atheist tonight." Of course, a few years later, God did honor his request, when Ingersoll died as every man does.

The Triune God does live. Atheists lash out at God and thus become fools. Edward Tabash, in a guest editorial in the *Los Angeles Times*, called God an "egomaniac" because He requires worship. God is not frazzled by the truth-suppressing hi-jinks of the atheists. The Bible announces: "The fool says in his heart there is no God" (Psalm 53:1). It is nonsense to say that God does not exist. If there is no God, we are all just molecules in motion and have no sense and no mind. We are just the random firing of chemicals in the brain. If our minds are composed of only physical matter, then our thoughts, as Doug Wilson wittily quipped in his debate with atheist Dan Barker, are no more than "brain gas." In that debate, Wilson went on to use an illustration of two soda-pop cans. If our minds are just the result of chemical reactions, then in the debate over soda-pop cans, God's existence can just as rightly be settled by shaking them simultaneously and afterward labeling one can "Atheism" and the other "Theism." The one that "fizzes the most wins."

If our minds were simply a fluctuation of proteins, neurotransmitters, and other biochemicals, then an intellectual debate is the equivalent of the chemical reactions that occur when one shakes a couple cans of soda. But that is foolishness. God does live. And because He lives, we can debate, and we can also account for the nonmaterial logic utilized in a debate. Atheists cannot account for debate inasmuch as they believe that the only thing that exists is matter.

Wishful Thinking Syndrome of Unbelief

The fact is, atheists know that God exists, but they want to malign and defy Him. John P. Koster, Jr., in his provocative book *The Atheist Syndrome,* convincingly demonstrates that most of the famous atheists had difficult or non-existent relationships with their earthly fathers. Thus they attempted to take out their hurt and frustration on the Father in Heaven by actively disbelieving in His existence. Koster documents that the ranting and raving of atheists such as Nietzsche, Freud, Huxley, Darwin, Ingersoll, Clarence Darrow, Hitler, and others were the result of an unhealthy relationship or lack of a relationship with their earthly fathers. This fueled their wishful thinking. Koster goes on to establish that these relationships led to mental illness in many of them, hence the "Atheist Syndrome." Koster brings this point to our attention:

> Materialists and atheists will, of course, be offended if we suggest that their heroes were actually insane, and their attack on God...was a deranged fantasy and not an explanation of scientific knowledge. But...Darwin, Thomas Huxley, Friedrich Nietzsche, and Sigmund Freud had many hallmarks of mental illness stamped on their personality. In point of fact, a careful study of their biographies in light of improved scientific knowledge may reveal not only that each man was mentally ill, but that each man suffered the same form of mental illness. It was this mental illness that led each of them to pervert science into an attack on God.[7]

Koster goes on to tell how the nineteenth-century Romantic poet Percy Bysshe Shelley rebelled against God because he was "tormented and beaten in a religiously-oriented school." Huxley and Freud revolted against the Almighty because they were "son-victims" and actually relieved their symptoms of mental illness by "raving against Christianity."

Huxley called his sedition against the Holy "crib-biting," and this raving produced physical and mental wellness and improved digestion. For Huxley, raging war against God cheered him up and improved his health. Koster reports how Freud, so diseased that his flesh was putrefying and rotting away, the stench repelling even his faithful dog, still kept his pen in hand to "hammer away on his final book, *Moses and Monotheism,* a book that assaults the foundations of the Biblical faith."

Paul C. Vitz's *The Faith of the Fatherless* demonstrates that, once children become "disappointed in or [lose] respect for [their] earthly father[s], belief in a heavenly father is impossible."[8] He goes on to reveal that all these famous atheists, from Nietzsche to Bertrand Russell, had either very troubled relationships with their fathers or no father at all in their lives. Hume's father died when he was two years old, Russell's when he was four, Sartre's and Camus' at one, and Arthur Schopenhauer's when he was a young teen. H. G. Wells, Madalyn Murray O'Hair, Stalin, and Freud all had difficult and troubling relationships with their earthly fathers. This led them to reject their heavenly Father because of their moral corruption, self-deception, and psychological instability. The two books listed above are fascinating and open up the emotional windows of those who actively and aggressively reject God and suppress His truth.

Many atheists are aggressive and blather away with forceful rhetoric. Their arguments are littered with inconsistencies and emotional declarations. Many public atheists rant against God and His dear Son. Most of them will dodge the challenge of a debate because of their fear of being refuted.

Crypto-Theism in Atheism

He [Jesus] is the image of the invisible God, the firstborn over all creation. For by Him all things were created, that are in heaven and that are on earth, visible and invisible, whether thrones or dominions or principalities or powers....And He is before all things, and in Him all things consist (Colossians 1:15-17).

Anti-theists believe in God; they know He exists. The ungodly do not know God in a saving way, in a covenant relationship. They know

Him through His attributes of providence, righteousness, justice, and goodness. They simply do not like Him. They really do not like Him. But not liking someone does not prove that he does not exist; not liking someone presupposes that he does. It is not so much that one cannot prove that God does or does not exist. God is not on trial. We do not have to go around proving that God exists. The true and living God lives, and everything we think, do, or say, presupposes that truth. Without God, one cannot make sense of anything, even the very question of God's existence. He has to exist, or we could not ponder that question or any other question. Everything around us can only be justified if God lives. All atheists know that God exists, because the atheist has to rest upon the Christian worldview to deny God's existence. The atheist uses logic, morality, and other nonmaterial truths to pronounce that God does not exist; when he does so, he affirms Christianity even as he attempts to refute it. The atheist cannot furnish the necessary *a priori* conditions for logic, reason, and truth. He claims he does not have enough evidence to believe in God. But there is evidence all around him—nothing but evidence. Anyone who opens his eyes believes in right and wrong and knows that God dwells in eternity. In the words of the old folk slogan, "It doesn't take a doctor of veterinary medicine to know when a dead skunk is on the road." Only with God as our foundation for life can we make sense out of the world. To allege that God does not exist requires God to exist to make the allegation. Greg Bahnsen demonstrates this truth with the following illustration:

> A person [who] argues that air doesn't exist will, all the while, breathe the air while he is arguing; yet, if what he said were true, he couldn't breathe at all. The theory that air doesn't exist would mean that you wouldn't be breathing. He could say you must be wrong about that because I'm arguing that air doesn't exist, and I am breathing. In reality, continuing to breathe disproves his theory, because he cannot account for his breathing. If he were right that air doesn't exist, it would be impossible to breathe.[9]

Obviously the atheist suppresses the truth in unrighteousness, so the job of the believer is to hold over him the reality that he cannot account for the laws of logic, ethics, and the pursuit of truth. When you ask the atheist, "Where does logic come from?" he will not have an answer. The laws of logic are not physical or material; they do not consist of atoms and molecules. The atheist attempts to demonstrate that only material substances exist in the universe, and when he uses nonmaterial logic he is refuting his own position.

The Transcendental Necessity of God

The sovereign God of scripture, speaking the universe into existence, sustaining and providentially controlling all things in the universe, is the only presupposition that can justify induction and the uniformity of the physical world. Thus God is the precondition for science and the investigation of the natural world. The true and living God must exist in order for us to account for the intricate and distinct interdependence of particulars in the united cosmos. That is the reason Anslem said, "I believe in order that I may understand." Van Til employed the following illustration:

> We cannot prove the existence of the beams underneath the floor if by proof you mean that they must be ascertainable in a way that we can see the chairs and the tables of the room. But the very idea of the floor as a support for the tables and chairs requires the idea of beams underneath. But, there would be no floor if no beams were underneath. Thus, there is absolute certain proof for the existence of God...Even non-Christians presuppose its truth while they verbally reject it. They need to presuppose the truth of Christianity to account for their own accomplishments.[10]

No one can make sense of anything in the world without presupposing the existence of God. When one attempts to construct a worldview on anything but Christianity, one will find, under philosophical scrutiny, that he cannot justify or account for anything in the cosmos. The person who denies the existence of God uses logic and reason to articulate his disbelief, yet there is no justification for his use of them. God is inescapable. Anyone attempting to escape the truth that God exists falls into a trap. This point is well made in Van Til's illustration of a man made of water, who is trying to climb out of the ocean by means of a ladder made of water. The man cannot get out of the water; nothing is left for him to stand on. In the same way, without God, one cannot make sense of anything. The atheist has nothing to stand on, climb, or grip.

Only the transcendent revelation of God can provide the necessary precondition for logic, science, morality, etc., in which case those who oppose the faith are reduced to utter foolishness and intellectually have nowhere to stand in objecting to Christian truth claims.[11]

A Dialogue with An Atheist

The conversation below is one I had with an aggressive atheist. It should be noted that Christians have all the rational weapons and ammunition. It's not my own intelligence that wins the debate; it's the truth from the out-workings of Scripture.

Mike: Hello, can I ask you a question?
Atheist: I'm busy, but go ahead.
Mike: Are you a Christian?
Atheist: No way. I don't believe in God or in other fairy-tales.
Mike: What do you believe in?
Atheist: I believe in evolution! I believe in science and in reason.
Mike: Why?
Atheist: Because they are true.
Mike: How do you know that?
Atheist: Well, I've seen pictures of fossils and geological columns that prove evolution is true.
Mike: Do you believe it is logical to believe in evolution?
Atheist: Of course. Only Neanderthals don't.
Mike: You said evolution is logical. Where does logic come from?
Atheist: What do you mean?
Mike: You state that you believe in evolution, and you must also believe that only the physical reality exists. My question to you is, if only the physical reality exists, where do the nonphysical, abstract, universal laws of logic come from? Can you buy them off the rack at Sears or pick them up in the field down the street?
Atheist: Uh, no.
Mike: There's your problem. Atheism can't supply the

foundation for logic. Every time you use logic, even when you attempt to prove that God doesn't exist, you are actually presupposing that God exits. Without God, you cannot prove anything or understand anything because you use logic in these pursuits. The precondition for logic is God.

Atheist: Well, I don't believe in God and I use logic all the time.

Mike: That's my point. All men everywhere are dependent on God in their use of logic and reason. You, as an atheist, can't justify your use of nonphysical logic.

Atheist: That's fine, but—

Mike: Let me ask you another question. Do you believe that it is wrong to murder and torture little children, and that it is wrong to burn down all the Amazon rain forests?

Atheist: Of course, it's wrong.

Mike: Why?

Atheist: It is wrong and you know it is.

Mike: Yes I do, but why is it wrong according to your worldview of evolution and the survival of the fittest? If a child is brutally murdered in your worldview, the little kid is just a non-survivor, just some physical matter that became un-animated. To affirm moral laws, one must presuppose the God of the Bible. God must be, or there can be no foundation for moral laws that are binding to everyone. Do you have a foundation for saying that something is right or wrong?

Atheist: I guess not.

Mike: Do you want to repent and turn to Christ?

Atheist: No, not today. You gave me many things to research.

Mike: Maybe we can get together later. Here, take this tract and an invitation to the church I attend.

Atheist: Thanks.

Ethics Must Come from God

The man who asserts a system of ethics without the God of the

Bible and His law has no foundation or justification for morals. Without God, murdering someone would just be the displacement of the atoms of the murder victim to another form. The victim is just a non-survivor. There is nothing wrong with adding water to dirt and making mud or raking leaves and tossing them into a fire. The atoms of the dirt and the leaves just take on different forms. The body of the murder victim, if only made up of physical atoms, would simply be changed into another form. Dirt, leaves, and a human being are, under the materialist worldview, all the same. God is the precondition for right and wrong, for justice and injustice. The famous atheist and libertine Bertrand Russell, in his unconvincing book *Why I'm Not A Christian,* mused: "The world I should wish to see would be one freed from the virulence of group hostilities and capable of realizing happiness for all." The question I would ask the former atheist, who died in 1972 (death makes one an instant theist), is: Why? Why should the world pursue that? The atheist has no justification for asserting or affirming any morals, any "oughts."

Moral laws are nonmaterial realities that presuppose a nonmaterial God who has the wisdom and authority to decree and enact them. Without God as the moral lawgiver, there cannot be nonmaterial moral laws. A holy, wise, and good God is the precondition for true, eternal, nonmaterial, and irreducible realities called moral laws. Materialistic atheism cannot account for irreducible nonmaterial entities that are to govern human behavior. Without an omnipotent, sovereign God issuing laws that are based on His perfect character, one has no motivation to obey the law simply because obedience is morally good. Leave God out of the picture and one only obeys the law because of the fear of possible penal sanction and civil punishment. When the civil authorities are not looking, one can steal, lie, cheat, and rape with impunity. There must be a sovereign and universal God to obey out of virtue and goodness alone. We have strong motivation to follow laws, when no one is looking, if the laws are intrinsically good and come from a good, all-seeing God, a God who commands humanity to love Him by obeying His commandments. When you take away the character and authority of God to enact laws, you are not obliged to obey them out of mere virtue and rightness.

Moral Law and Truth

Everyone has to acknowledge some form of moral law (for the few who try to deny moral law, see the argument below). The precondition of moral law is the God of the Bible. Here is a simple syllogism to demonstrate that God is inescapable:

1. To postulate that there are no moral absolutes is to make a truth claim.
2. A truth claim presupposes moral absolutes; hence, there are moral absolutes.
3. An objective moral law can only exist if an immutable, absolute moral Lawgiver exists.
4. Therefore, God, the immutable absolute Lawgiver, exists. It is impossible for Him not to exist.

If one denies the premise, it is impossible for that denial to be true because it would be self-refuting. If the denial were true, one would be faced with the impossible problem of morally demanding that others "ought" to affirm the denial against an absolute moral law. Thus the denial itself becomes an absolute moral law. If one does not have to affirm the denial absolutely, then it is not universally and absolutely true, and thus it is false. The denial of moral absolutes is self-defeating; the denial of morality presupposes morality. The attempt to deny absolute moral law affirms it. To deny fixed morality is illogical, meaningless, and self-defeating. There must be an objective, absolute Lawgiver. If one tries to fall back on the canard that "all things are meaningless," one commits philosophical suicide. If all things were meaningless, then that would include the statement itself that all things are meaningless. It is impossible for all things to be meaningless.

Personal Identity Presupposes God

> Then God said, Let Us make man in Our image, according to Our likeness (Genesis 1:26).

> If the world were not as scripture says it is, if the natural man's knowledge were not actually rooted in the creation and providence of God, then there would be no knowledge....The non-Christians have made and now make discoveries about the state of the universe simply because the universe is what Christ says it is. The unbelieving scientist borrows or steals the Christian principle of creation and providence every time

he says that an "explanation" is possible, for he knows he cannot account for an "explanation" on his own.[12]

The nonbeliever cannot account for the intelligibility of anything, even his own personal identity. When someone says, "I'm Ernie," and means that he is the same "Ernie" as the person in his high school yearbook named "Ernie," he is borrowing from the Christian worldview. Only Christianity can give us a reason to be certain we are who we are. Our physical bodies change every moment and every day. Human beings lose one-sixtieth of an ounce of respiratory moisture and sweat every minute; there is a net loss every second, meaning that humans physically change every moment. Hence, under a materialist worldview, I am not the same person I was a second ago. The skin replaces itself once a month. The stomach lining is replaced every five days. The cells in the liver are replaced every six weeks, and the skeleton about every three months. The body of every human being changes constantly. The cells of a human body are in a constant state of flux and are always being modified. In one year the average person has ninety-eight percent of his atoms exchanged for new ones. In seven years' time every atom in a person's body has been replaced. Thus the person is a new and completely different being within the worldview of the materialist atheist (faster if you visit the dentist frequently).

The atheist affirms that only the material world exists, claiming that nothing spiritual or nonmaterial exists. After seven years everyone is a different person. So the atheist cannot account for personal identity. By his standard of a materialist world, everyone is a different person after seven years, because every atom has been replaced by a new one. The atheist, under his worldview, would not be married to the same woman he married nine years ago. They are totally different physically, due to the complete replacement of bodily atoms every seven years. If he has a child over the age of seven, then by the atheist's standard he is not the same child who was born to them. Therefore, if he wanted to be consistent in his worldview, he should throw away all baby pictures along with his wedding album. Every molecule in his body has changed. And in a materialist world, he is a different person. But he will not throw away his baby pictures or his wedding album, because he is basing much of his life on the Christian worldview. The atheist husband still hugs his wife without being unfaithful to her. He will still take his kid to the park and buy him a balloon. But he will not buy the stranger who is next to him a balloon. The atheist knows that his child is the same child who was born to him years before. He lives much of his life on the Christian worldview without even recognizing it.

Physical Change: A Boat and A Bob

A man named Bob builds a fishing boat and names it Dolly Mae. A couple of years later he replaces all the wood because the color is fading. He throws the wood in a pile on the side yard. Later Bob replaces all the nails and metal binders with new ones. He tosses them in the side yard with the wood. His friend sees the wood and nails and asks Bob if he can have them to build a canoe. Bob lets him have them, and the friend builds a canoe with all the wood, nails, and metal from the boat. Which vessel should be named Dolly Mae? This paradox exposes the problem that atheists have with human identity. The first boat has none of its original parts—the canoe has them all, but with a different shape. Hence, neither vehicle is the original; they have both changed. The first has changed in its physical parts and the second in its shape and design. In the materialist view of life, humans who lose body parts to disease or accidents are not the same people they were before the loss.

The Christian professes that man is made in God's image. We all have what scholars have called *sensus deitatis*, a sense of God or deity. We know who we are by looking at God and His revelation. God's word announces who we are—our unchanging personal identity. Humans have a personal identity that transcends the physical world. Christians can hold their ten-year-old child's hand and hug their grandparents and remain consistent within their own worldview. When the anti-theist performs these types of caring actions towards his loved ones, he is being inconsistent with his presuppositions.

The atheist knows that men have souls; and although they deny this obvious truth, they live as though it were true. If personal identity did not have a nonmaterial aspect, anyone who had lost a couple of limbs in an accident, had his skin burned off in a fire, or lost a couple of organs would not be the same person. His identity would change in a materialist's worldview. Suppose a man lost all his skin due to a chemical accident. That same man had to have his kidneys replaced due to an adverse reaction to the medication. He got so depressed, he drank in excess and had to receive a new liver. One day, he was so despondent that he hurled himself out of his third-story window and lost all his limbs. New technology provided him with new limbs, new organs, and new skin. With almost his entire physical body replaced, is he still his mother's son? Is he still his wife's husband? Is he still the father of his little girl? Is he still the same man? The answer is yes—yes because he has a spirit and he has a soul. He is more than the sum of his physical parts; he is a human being created in the image of God. That is another reason that the anti-theist cannot live consistently within his own worldview. He must borrow from the Christian worldview because Christianity is true and is the basis of all truth. Unless God is presupposed, there is no objective, unchanging reason to value all men and women. In the atheist's worldview, a human being is just a bipedal blob of water and protein. There is no moral reason for the world to esteem a human being as anything more important than a bumblebee. Nevertheless, we see atheists affirming the dignity and value of man; when they do this they are living contrary to their own worldview. For the non-theist there is nothing in the world, including the world itself, that can be justified. There is no accounting for value, truth, or science without the God revealed in scripture. God has spoken. He has revealed Himself. This is the reason we value humanity and can make sense out of this world. Christianity must be true, because it alone makes the world intelligible and knowledge possible.

Do the Crime and Do the Time?

To reject the notion that man has a spirit has implications for the penal system as well. According to the atheist's worldview, all that exists is the material world; if this were true, after seven years the state should let all murderers out of prison. Remember that they have had all their atoms replaced by new ones. Therefore, they are now different people, according to the materialist worldview of atheism. The materialist atheist should not kiss his wife goodbye if they have been married for over seven years. Materially speaking, they are totally different people, so he is not kissing the same woman he married. He should not choose to buy his nine-year old son an ice cream in preference to the stranger next to him. To live consistently within a materialist philosophy is ridiculous and confusing. We sip champagne on our tenth anniversary with our spouses and buy birthday presents for our twelve-year-old daughter because the Christian worldview is true; it is impossible for it not to be.

In Christ are hidden all the treasures of wisdom and knowledge (Colossians 2:3).

If there were no God, one could not ever say, "I do not believe in God." One could not say, "I," because there would be no "I." One could not make any assertion at all. Only if God exists can one account for self-identity and justify any personal assertion. It is not just that Christianity makes better sense in describing human experience; Christianity is the precondition for making sense out of any item in the world. Without it, one could not account for his selfhood or the universe in which he lives. No one has ultimate authority to assert that he understands anything in the entire cosmos. We are not to employ slick arguments to verify that God lives. God is the ultimate reference point and the judge of all things. His word is foundational, necessary, and self-authenticating. What God says was, or is, or will be. We do not have to scramble around trying to prove God with ingenious arguments that can dazzle men. God is the foundation for all meaning, purpose, morals, and rationality. God alone makes any rational argument possible and reasonable. He is the source of all truth, order, logic, mathematics, goodness, beauty, and philosophy. The reality of these things is absolute and certain proof that God lives. Bahnsen put it well when he said:

> The Christian offers the self-attesting Christ to the world as the only foundation upon which a man must stand to give any "reasons" for anything at all. The whole notion of "giving reasons" is completely destroyed by any ontology other than the Christian one. The Christian claims that only after accepting the Biblical scheme of things will any man be able to understand and account for his own rationality.[13]

I Do Not Exist!

There are those who claim that they themselves do not exist; such a notion is impossible. In stating that "I" do not exist, one must employ the word and presuppose the reality "I." A man's personal identity is a necessary precondition to assert that "he" does not exist. Just as logic is a necessary precondition, though insufficient to explain the world, personal identity is necessary though insufficient to explain reality. Thus personal existence is undeniable. To deny one's existence is to presuppose one's existence. The problem for the unbeliever is that he cannot account for personal identity. The same line of argument can be used to refute those who claim that others do not exist. When they proclaim, "You do not exist!" ask them, "Who does not exist?" They must either say "You" or shut up. Thus they refute themselves.

The Only Living and True God

And God said to Moses, "I AM WHO I AM." And He said, "Thus you shall say to the children of Israel, 'I AM has sent me to you'" (Exodus 3:14).

An atheist who asserts that the material world alone exists, devoid of all spiritual and abstract entities, cannot account for his use of nonphysical logic in his reasoning. Logic is abstract, transcendent, universal, and nonmaterial. Only the Christian worldview can supply the necessary preconditions for the nonmaterial, unchanging, and universal laws of logic. The laws of logic cannot be found in a box or a closet. One cannot purchase a set of the laws of logic on sale at a store; they are not concrete and physical. Only the transcendent, unchanging, universal, and nonmaterial God can provide the necessary preconditions for transcendent, universal, unchanging, and nonphysical logic. Thus it is impossible for the atheistic scientist to be correct in declaring that nothing exists except the physical world. That declaration is itself nonmaterial, and thus, false. It is impossible for God not to exist.

The unbeliever's worldview collapses under its own weight because he cannot justify or account for the rational world. I will reiterate this fact throughout the book until you can anticipate my words. I have written in this redundant manner because humanity has a strong propensity for self-deception. The unbeliever will deny all the evidence for theism, and deceive himself, so that he may sleep better at night. We must put away self-deception. The Gallup Poll of February 2002 (six months after Muslim extremists destroyed the World Trade Center, damaged the Pentagon, and murdered 3000 people) was a survey of the Islamic world. Most of the Muslims polled—the great majority—believed that the act of crashing planes into the World Trade Center and Pentagon was morally justified. But most Islamic countries also did not believe that al Qaeda terrorists flew the planes into the World Trade Center and Pentagon in the first place. The massive Muslim denial of the wickedness of these crimes, and their continued deception in believing that Muslims did not participate in these atrocities, illustrates the human trait of self-deception. Humans willingly and tenaciously desire to hold on to what they know is false to make themselves feel better. Few people want to examine difficult truths about themselves and their false god. Without the Christian God, the unbeliever cannot make sense out of any thought, word, or deed in heaven or on earth.

False Deities Cannot Help

The false gods of other religions cannot help anyone. These gods do not exist, for they are made in the image of man. The only God whose existence is not contingent on men is the God of the Bible. The Mormon gods, the Hindu gods, the Islamic god, and the Sikh god do not have necessary existence. There are worlds in which these gods would not exist. They are not necessary in all possible worlds. They are not logically and ontologically necessary beings. Only the Triune God of scripture is the precondition for the intelligibility of this world, or any world one could imagine. He is necessary, not contingent. The entire cosmos is dependent upon God. Yahweh is necessary; it would be impossible for the Lord God not to exist. The Almighty is all-sufficient, all-knowing, and all-powerful in His sovereignty. God is not dependent on anything in any world. The world is completely dependent on Him. All existence, all opinions, and all debate presuppose the God who spoke from the burning bush and declared to Moses and future generations: "I AM THAT I AM."

Notes

[1] Ray Comfort, *Hell's Best Kept Secret* (Springdale, PA: Whitaker House, 1989), p. 120.

[2] C. S. Lewis, *Surprised by Joy* (New York: Harcourt, Brace & Co.,1955), p. 211.

[3] C. S. Lewis *The Quotable Lewis,* Eds. Martindale & Root (Wheaton, IL: Tyndale House, 1989), p. 60.

[4] Ibid.

[5] Greg Bahnsen, *Van Til's Apologetic* (Phillipsburg, NJ: P & R, 1998), p. 494.

[6] David Hume, *A Treatise of Human Nature* (Oxford: Oxford Press, 2000), pp. 150-151.

[7] John P. Koster, Jr., *The Atheist Syndrome* (Brentwood, TN: Wolgemuth & Hyatt, 1989), p. 12.

[8] Paul Vitz, *Faith of the Fatherless* (Dallas: Spence, 1999), p. 16.

[9] Greg Bahnsen, *Covenant Media Tape* (Irvine, CA: Covenant Media), 1985.

[10] Cornelius Van Til, *The Defense of Faith* (Phillipsburg, NJ: P & R, 1955), p. 120.

[11] Bahnsen, p. 676.

[12] Bahnsen, p. 696.

[13] Bahnsen, pp. 696-697.

CHAPTER FOUR

AGNOSTICISM: IGNORANT AND LOST

You're worried about being lost, Palmer. You're worried about not being central, not the reason the universe was created. There's plenty of order in the universe. Gravitation, electromagnetism, quantum mechanics....[T]hey all involve laws.[1]

The knowledge of God is inherent in man. It is there by virtue of his creation in the image of God.[2]

Agnosticism is completely self-contradictory. And it is self-contradictory not only upon the assumption of the truth of theism, but it is self-contradictory upon its own assumptions. Agnosticism wants to hold that it is reasonable to refrain from thorough epistemological speculations because they cannot lead to anything. But to assume this attitude, Agnosticism has itself made the most tremendous intellectual assertion that could be made about ultimate things. In the second place, Agnosticism is epistemologically self-contradictory on its own assumptions because its claim to make no assertion about ultimate reality rests upon a most comprehensive assertion about ultimate reality.[3]

Agnostics have many different starting points. Some claim that no one can know anything about God. Of course, such a statement itself claims knowledge about God. The agnostic who arbitrarily supposes we cannot know anything about God in fact says something very important about God—that He is unknowable.

Not only does he have no philosophical or logical basis to make such a claim, the claim self-destructs and implodes from within. The agnostic, though attempting to confess ignorance of theology, has a rather elaborate theology. His assertion that we can know nothing about God in fact builds a prodigious theological system. This system asserts that we cannot know that God is omnipotent, omnipresent, loving, just, and sovereign. Agnostics also presume to know that God has not revealed Himself to humanity, implying that He is either too weak in power or too indifferent in His concern for His creatures. Agnostics claim a lot about God; as you can see, they have an intricate theological system.

Open But Unconvinced

Another type of agnostic admits he does not know whether God exists, but says that others might. The word "agnostic" is not a label that anyone should desire. The word comes from the Greek word meaning ignorant and without knowledge. In one sense the term is fitting. Anyone who tries to hoodwink others into believing that they do not know whether God exists is ignorant and self-deceived. The Bible clearly teaches that they do know that God is but that they actively suppress that knowledge. I can affirm this fact not just as doctrine but in practice, since I have had the wonderful opportunity to speak with dozens of agnostics. Their suppression of knowledge will be evident in some of the conversations presented later.

Self-deception

"Dare to know" is the challenge issued by Kant. The agnostic runs from this charge and remains locked into self-deception. He knows that God exists, but he does not like Him. Hell, judgment, and all that nasty stuff are not for him. He lives on wishful thinking and deceives himself by suppressing the truth of God in unrighteousness. He is like the man who in the summer of 2001 used what Coast Guard Cmdr. Dee Norton described as "poor judgment": He strapped on homemade "water-walking shoes" and decided to walk on the Pacific Ocean from California to Hawaii, a distance of more than two thousand miles. The amazing thing was, he did get about ten miles—until his shoes started taking in too much water. He radioed for help and was rescued. This man should be enshrined in the Self-Deception Hall of Fame. He actually believed he could cross the high seas by walking across the Pacific Ocean with extra-large "shoes." However, the unbeliever has more reasons to trust God than a man has for realizing he can not step-walk across the deep blue sea.

As we proclaim the gospel, we should remind ourselves of the great tendency of unregenerate man to deceive himself. Man's propensity to fall for and embrace self-deception found its height following the wicked acts committed on September 11, 2001. The great majority of Muslims in over twenty countries did not believe that other Muslims flew planes into the Twin Towers and the Pentagon. They claimed not to have seen any "smoking gun," and that the attack was all a "Jewish plot." Months later the "smoking gun" was revealed in the form of the Bin Laden tapes that were released. The tapes showed Bin Laden bragging about his murderous acts on 9-11. However, the great majority of the Muslims polled still believed the wicked acts were not committed by Muslims. The self-deception goes even farther—the same *USA Today* opinion poll revealed that most of the Islamic world did not believe that the terrorism committed against America on September 11th was "morally wrong." Duplicity like this should send shivers down the backs of world leaders. Muslim countries lead the world in self-deception, but all unregenerate men have a similar capacity and desire to deceive themselves. Often people do not want to believe the bad news even if it is there. Thus many of us can live under the nurture, warmth, and glow of God's benevolent common grace and yet assert that He does not exist. The Christian does not have to live under the dark umbrella of self-deception; he has certainty. Unless Christianity is presupposed, there is no proof for anything. Christianity is the very foundation for proof and the discovery of truth.

When the non-theist is confronted with the truth, frequently he will behave like the little boy in Bahnsen's analogy who, mad at his parents for punishing him, hides under his blanket and declares that his mom and dad don't exist. The reality is that his parents exist, whether he likes it or not. He can attempt to deceive and lie to himself in a futile effort to make himself feel better. Bahnsen uses this analogy to illustrate that the unbeliever is doing the same thing. He is mad at God for being God. He is angry about the coming judgment of his personal sins, so he hides under his blanket of unbelief, hoping that God is not there. Others hope that God will just go away. Thus every day the unbeliever must try really hard to convince himself that the Triune God does not exist. Nonetheless, if one is hiding or rebelling in the open, God still dwells in majesty.

An Encounter at the University

Mike: Hello, do you have a moment to take a survey?

Phil: No. I'm late.

Mike: Can I walk you to your car?

Phil: Fine.

Mike: Are you an agnostic or a theist?

Phil: I'm an atheist.

Mike: So you don't believe in God?

Phil: Well, not really. Uh, I—well, I actually do believe in God.

Mike: Were you raised Christian, Muslim, or Roman Catholic?

Phil: I was raised by two of those you listed. I was born and raised in Africa. My father's a Muslim and my mother a Catholic. I went to Catholic schools because those were the only schools in my area. I don't believe in any of those religions. I've investigated religions and found all of them lacking.

Mike: I'm sure you know the main difference between Christianity and Islam is the person of Christ. Christianity asserts that Jesus is God's Son and Islam denies this.

Phil: Yes.

Mike: Have you heard of the evidence for the resurrection of Christ?

Phil: Yes, but—umm, we had missionaries from Europe teach us in school.

Mike: You then realize that the resurrection was first proclaimed in Jerusalem, the very town of Christ's death and burial. And that Roman guards secured the grave of Christ. After three days the tomb was empty, and the followers of Jesus announced that He had risen from the dead. All the disciples, except Judas, died or were persecuted for believing and proclaiming that Christ rose on the third day.

	Nonbiblical writers of that generation recount the resurrection of Christ, including the Jewish historian Josephus. Muhammad stayed dead. Jesus rose. Can you see the contrast?
Phil:	Uh-mm.
Mike:	Let me give you the argument from the impossibility of the contrary. The God of the Bible is the foundation and precondition for all reason, logic, and morality. Without the God of the Bible you cannot account for rationality, logic, or ethics. Everyone going to school here is using reason and logic in their studies. Yet if they say that God doesn't exist, they can't account for reason and logic. They can't tell us where the logic they use for studying came from, or the reasoning they use in trying to assert that God doesn't exist. For them to make a logical assertion, they have to stand on Christian assumptions. Reason and logic are laws, and they're not physical or material. You can't go down the street and buy them on sale. The laws of logic are abstract, transcendent, universal and nonphysical. The laws of logic are always true. "A" can't be "A" and "Non-A" at the same time in the same way, always. If the Christian worldview isn't true, then logic is impossible. Only Christianity supplies the foundation necessary for logic, science, and mathematics. No non-Christian system of thought can furnish a foundation for the law of non-contradiction; thus, those false systems of thought are self-contradictory. The true and living Creator is the precondition for all knowledge, proof, math, evidence, and logic. The nonphysical, transcendent and immutable God supplies the necessary preconditions for the use of nonphysical, transcendent, universal, and immutable laws of reason. Thus, the contrary of Christianity is impossible because all other worldviews fall into absurdity since they're self-refuting.
Phil:	O.K.
Mike:	The laws of logic come from God. Since we use logic, we affirm God, even when we're attempting

to deny Him. Logic presupposes the God of the Bible. God's nature is the only way to account for the laws of logic. Now, there is another matter to ponder:you've made mistakes and I've made mistakes. We have all sinned and have broken God's law.

Phil: Yes.

Mike: What religion has an answer to the problem of sin? You have admitted that you have sinned; so have I. The problem for us is: God is Holy and perfect; Heaven is perfect and we aren't. How does one who is not perfect get into a perfect heaven?

Phil: Uh-mm.

Mike: In all the world's religions the only answer for the remission of sins is Christ's atoning work on the cross.

Phil: Um.

Mike: Christ died on the cross to remove the believer's sins so that we could make it to heaven by grace alone. Do you follow me?

Phil: Yes, I follow you. Jesus died to be merciful and to take care of God's justice.

(At this point we made it to his truck. The providence of God was clearly displayed because he discovered that he had lost his keys, giving me an opportunity to walk him back and expound more on the person and work of Christ. It was a long walk in both directions. I first asked him whether he needed any assistance to find his keys, gave him some gospel tracts and a church invitation, then started where I had left off.)

Mike: So, the infinite justice of God...

Phil: Uh-mm.

Mike: If God is just, how can He be merciful?

Phil: Uh-mm.

Mike: In other words, you wouldn't want an earthly judge in our world to be merciful with the exclusion of justice. Suppose a judge had in his court rapists, murderers, and thieves. You wouldn't want that judge to say, "I'm going to be merciful today. You guys are all forgiven. Just go." You would be outraged. Muslims, Jews, and other people would say that men make it to heaven because God forgives them. If you ask them on what basis God forgives them, they would say, He is merciful. But if He is merciful without justice, then He is not really good, honorable, and just. If a civil judge freed a courtroom full of rapists and murderers because he said he wanted to be merciful, society would be outraged. They would say he is unjust, evil, and morally corrupt. If one says God forgives everyone based solely on His mercy, one has a God who is evil, unrighteous, and unjust.

Phil: O.K.

Mike: Only Christianity solves the dilemma of applying both justice and mercy to the sinner. God has been merciful to us by sending His Son to die for us on the cross, satisfying God's justice. Christ paid the price for the believer's sins. The penalty was paid on the cross. God acted in mercy and carried out perfect justice. Non-Christian religions have a god who gives mercy, but doesn't execute justice. And God is infinitely more just than any judge in the entire world. So the dilemma is, how does a world religion solve the problem of the tension between mercy and justice? A god who says, "I forgive you on account of nothing" isn't a good, holy or just god. The God of the Bible is holy, just, good, and merciful — Him alone.

Phil: Uh-mm.

Mike: A god, like Allah, who forgives without executing justice is a capricious and arbitrary god.

Phil: You can't know what God will do.

Mike: I'm saying, if that's your god, he's capricious and arbitrary. You can say he does that, but that is your god. That can be your proposition, you can say that, but then, the nature of the god you're proclaiming is a god who is arbitrary and capricious. Only the Biblical God is merciful and not arbitrary. He sent His Son, an eternal perfect being, to pay an eternal

	price. And all the sins of those who come to Him are forgiven. Do you follow me?
Phil:	Yes, I follow you.
Mike:	There is no other world religion that has answers to those problems; only Christianity supplies the answers. Christ offers justification. When you put your faith in Him alone, God declares you forensically righteous. Your sins are removed, and God imputes the righteousness of Christ to the believer.
Phil:	What is the main thing you are trying to tell me?
Mike:	God is sovereignly in control of the whole world, and for some reason He set up this time for you and me to talk for a moment. He even arranged for you to lose your keys, so you would come to understand that you're a sinner. We have all sinned against God's law, and I'm here to say that Christ is the only solution to the problem of God being merciful and just to sinners. If you turn and trust Him, He'll forgive you.
Phil:	He will forgive me?
Mike:	Yes, because of what He did on the cross.
Phil:	So, you're telling me that God is merciful.
Mike:	Yes. You see, He is merciful and just. He met the requirements of justice and mercy on the cross; only the Christian God has done that. He alone is the true and living God. He is calling you to turn from sin and believe in Jesus Christ. It's been good talking with you.
Phil:	Yes, it has.
Mike:	Let's get together again in the near future.
Phil:	O.K. Take care.
Mike:	You too.

Man Has A Purpose

Therefore, whether you eat or drink, or whatever you do, do all to the glory of God (1 Corinthians 10:31).

God gives man purpose. Hope, faith, and meaning come from God and His revealed will. The Westminster Catechism sums up the Bible and instructs us that "the chief end of man is to glorify God and enjoy Him forever." The man who refuses to believe in God cannot find any ultimate purpose or meaning. In the agnostic worldview, everything is heading for oblivion, since there is no personal God. The second law of thermodynamics guarantees that the whole universe is heading for a cosmic burnout. The universe is running down like a clock. And the sun, the stars, and the galaxies will be extinguished in a death by distilled energy. In the distant future there will be a total burnout of the entire universe. All the schemes, fancies, and accomplishments of mankind will be like "cosmic snowmen" who melt into nothingness at the coming of the summer. The moon, the planets, the quasars, and all the solar systems will be snuffed out, and with them will go all the accomplishments and intentions of mankind. The law of entropy guarantees that, without God and His clear purpose, everything will evaporate into unusable energy. All existence will be as though it had never been and will bear the final seal of nothingness as it dwindles to the lowest level of energy. All industry, education, art, and civilization will be as if they had never been. The eternal mark of meaninglessness will be infused across the vacant plain of the former cosmos. All the hopes, dreams, and loves of the world will fizzle into the oblivion of raw energy as if they had never taken place. This is the ultimate prophecy of the atheistic materialist: A universe without a purpose meandering toward a terminal blackout.

The Purposeless Purpose of Eastern Religions

Mankind is unique and has a God-given purpose. Rocks will never learn algebra; cucumbers will never strive to play Mozart. The human soul is always searching. Mankind knows there must be something more out there or up there. Something transcendent must exist, or we would never ask questions about purpose. Is this all there is? Many rich, powerful, and famous people live lives that do not satisfy their restless hearts. Many of them become so despondent that they commit suicide to try to relieve their pain. All their toys, all their wealth, and all their publicity will leave them without real purpose if they deny God.

The good news is that God has a plan and a purpose. The Eastern religions, such as Buddhism and Hinduism, do not have temporal or eternal good news. The ultimate goal of Buddhism is to escape into Nirvana and lose onself; one's purpose is to become nothing and know nothing. Pondering and believing such a thing can only bring despair and weaken one's moral fortitude. Hinduism teaches that man's goal is to break the karmic cycle and become one small drop of water that falls into the great ocean of god. Hinduism's central doctrine of reincarnation cannot supply hope; its goal is for everyone to dissolve into oneness. Because this world is an illusion, one must come back to the earth as another person or a cockroach. One must experience eternal release and just fall into the ocean of being and lose personality and meaning— one's self, family, and soul. The ultimate purpose of the Eastern religions is to have no purpose—which can only envelop the soul in hopelessness and despair. Scripture declares that the one true and living God has a marvelous purpose for all His children. Our ultimate purpose is to honor Christ the Son. Our eternal goal is to honor, worship, and delight in God forever. The universe may end in a cosmic burnout, but the one who created it has built a place for all His children, a heavenly home that will never perish or burn out. An eternal home with God is a grand purpose and a great destination of complete satisfaction.

Will the Real Atheist Please Stand Up?

The Bible makes it clear that there are no real agnostics or atheists. All men know that God exists, and they are attempting to suppress this truth in unrighteousness. Philosophically there cannot be atheists. For one to propose that God does not exist, anywhere at any time, one would have to know all things and be omnipresent, eternal, and infinite—and that would make one God. Thus the only person in the universe who could possibly not believe in God would be God. One would have to be God to be a true atheist; and that is theoretically, logically, and rationally absurd.

Important Issues Discussed with An Agnostic

Mike: Are you a Christian?
Agnostic: No, I don't know whether God exists and neither do you!
Mike: How do you know that?
Agnostic: Uh, well, I don't care.

Mike: Do you use logic and reason in your life?

Agnostic: Yes, everybody does.

Mike: Where does logic come from?

Agnostic: The brain.

Mike: How do you know that?

Agnostic: I don't know.

Mike: Only God can supply the necessary preconditions for logic. Deny God and you have to deny logic, which would be absurd.

Agnostic: Why does God have to exist for logic to be real?

Mike: Christianity is the only worldview that supplies human reason a base for proper function. No non-Christian system of thought can furnish a foundation for the law of non-contradiction. Thus those systems of thought can only offer a self-contradictory worldview. All non-Christian thought results in futility because of the internal contradictions they supply. Thus, the contrary of Christianity is impossible because every anti-Christian worldview falls into a moronic ditch. They're all internally self-contradictory and lead to conclusions that contradict their own terms. Christianity alone supplies the preconditions to make reality intelligible. The Biblical truth is that without God nothing can make sense. The true and living God is the precondition for the intelligibility of reality and the understanding of all human experiences.

Agnostic: I'm not sure I know what you're trying to say.

Mike: Unless you believe in the Triune God and His revealed word, you can't consistently and logically believe in anything else. God is the precondition for all argument, proof, evidence, and reason. It's impossible for God not to exist because He is the precondition for all intelligent thought. The nonphysical, universal, and unchanging God alone provides the necessary preconditions for the use of nonphysical, universal, invariant laws of logic. To argue at all, you must presuppose that God lives because you're using logic. All non-believing thought cannot supply the necessary preexisting foundations for the laws of logic; this results in futility because of the internal contradictions they supply. Thus, the contrary of Christianity is impossible because all contrary worldviews fall into absurdity since they're self-contradictory and lead to conclusions that contradict their own assertions.

Agnostic: This sounds interesting but I like my life and there may be other worldviews just as true.

Mike: Only the true God can supply all the absolutely necessary preconditions for all human experience. Christianity is the only worldview that supplies a foundation for human reason. Non-Christian systems of thought cannot furnish a foundation for the law of non-contradiction; thus, those systems of thought can only offer a self-contradictory worldview. God is the precondition for all argument, proof, evidence and reason. It's impossible for God not to exist. The Trinity is the precondition for all intelligent communication, because all human communication requires the use of the laws of logic. The omnipresent, transcendent, nonphysical, and unchanging God alone provides the necessary underlying conditions for the use of nonphysical, universal, and unchanging laws of logic. To argue at all, you must assume that God lives. Non-believing thought cannot supply the necessary preconditions underpinning the laws of logic. Thus, it results in futility because of the internal contradictions they supply. Without God nothing can make sense. The true and living God is the precondition for the intelligibility of reality and the understanding of all human experiences.

Agnostic: I don't buy it.

Mike: Whether you affirm God or not, He still lives. And He demands perfection in keeping His moral law and you have broken His law. You need a Savior. Christ died on the cross and rose again. I call on you to turn to and trust in Christ.

Agnostic: I don't want to. I got to go.

A Meeting with A Buddhist

Mike: Do you believe in Christ?

Student (a Buddhist man born in Japan):   Well, no, I'm a Buddhist.

Mike: Have you heard that Christ came to the earth from heaven, died on a cross for our sins, and rose again on the third day?

Student: Why, sure.

Mike: Are you attracted to that?

Student: You know, sometimes some people in Japan avoid a certain number because of Christ.

Mike: I didn't know that. The Bible instructs us that all men have made mistakes and have sinned. We've all failed and broken God's law. We've worshipped other gods, put things above God, used His name in vain, at times lied, stolen, and had sexual relations outside marriage. We have not kept all the Lord God's commandments. We are not perfect. Heaven is perfect. Only Christ's death on the cross can remove our mistakes, and sins, so we can go to a perfect heaven when we die.

Student: O.K.

Mike: If one believes Buddha or Muhammad and tries to follow their teachings, these actions can't remove their sins. Christ died on the cross for the remission of our sins. Do you understand what Jesus did?

Student: Well...I don't know.

Mike: Every person on this planet has sinned. Heaven is perfect, so without Christ, how would an imperfect person enter heaven?

Student: Well—

Mike: Everybody on the planet has sinned. What answer do you have? I'm not perfect, you are not perfect. How do you get to heaven?

Student: I don't believe that believing in Christ is important. Even the Buddha is not perfect, you know.

Mike: But Christ was, and He rose again from the dead.

Student: I don't know. I don't know that Christ was perfect.

Mike: Have you ever heard of the prophecies of Christ?

Student: No.

Mike: There were over three hundred prophecies of Christ's birth, life, mission, and death. These prophecies were written down before He came to the earth to identify His person and purpose. These were written down before He was born. The Bible gave us over three hundred prophecies: The location of His birth, how He was to be born, the exact time He would enter Jerusalem, how He would die, and that He would rise again from the dead. These predictions, and hundreds of others, all came true in the life of Jesus. This identifies Jesus as the Son of God. No other founder of a religion had numerous prophecies written down in advance of his birth.

Student: Well—

Mike: The main truth you need to know is that the God of the Bible is the precondition for the intelligibility of this world. You can't make sense out of anything in reality without Christianity.

Student: Uh—

Mike: Imagine I had a neighbor who knocked on my door late one night and told me that a Pepsi can spoke with him. He tells me that the Pepsi can told him to write down what it was saying. My friend says, "Mike, this is the answer to finding God. This can spoke with me and had me write out this book. If I follow the can, I'll find peace, wellness, and paradise when I die." If he said this, I would ask him, "How do you know this is true?" He says, "Look, I have this book. I transcribed it. Just believe and then follow it, and you'll have peace and eternal life." I ask him, "How can I know that it was God who spoke to you from the Pepsi can?" He again shows me the book and testifies. I tell him that is not good enough. There are hundreds of alleged holy books that claim to be from God. Except for the Bible, none of them stand out, and none of them offer me valid reasons to believe they are from God. Their proponents assert empty claims. Christ is different.

He doesn't make vain assertions. He is *the* truth.
Christianity is the ultimate basis for reason, logic,
morality, and the ability for us to make assertions.
Every founder from every religion, except Christ,
is just like my friend with the Pepsi can.

Student: Yes.

Mike: Are you interested in becoming a Christian?

Student: Uh, no.

Mike: Would you like to visit our church?

Student: Yes.

Mike: Here's an invitation. It has a map and directions to
the church. I hope I'll see you soon.

The Christian Has Certainty

These things I have written to you who believe in the name of
the Son of God, that you may know that you have eternal life,
and that you may continue to believe in the name of the Son
of God (1 John 5:13).

Christianity is absolutely certain. As reported by the *New York Times*, philosopher Richard Swinburne used Baye's Theorem to calculate that the probability of the resurrection of Jesus Christ was a "whopping 97%." Swinburne is a very intelligent man, but God is not a "probable" theory. God is not even 97% certain to exist. God does exist, and we can have complete certainty of His sovereign being. Job announces that he *knows* his Redeemer lives (Job 19:25). Paul declares that he *knows* in whom he has believed (2 Timothy 1:12). It is impossible for the Christian worldview to be false. I am saved by grace alone, and I have certainty through the Holy Spirit and God's true word. It is impossible for God not to exist. Calvin said that scripture was so "clear and certain it cannot be overthrown either by men or angels."

Everyone must hold to some universal and certain claims. The agnostic may deny certainty, but certain and universal claims are unavoidable. The agnostic claims that no one can know anything for certain, is itself a claim for certainty. The agnostic makes nonsense of human experience and falls into W. V. Quine's mire of the "baffling tangle of relations between our sensory stimulation and our scientific theory of the world." Positing the lack of certain knowledge makes nonsense of human experience. If the Christian worldview is not true, then knowledge is impossible; but if knowledge is impossible, one could not know it because that itself would be knowledge. Christianity is unavoidable, since one must rely on the Christian worldview to try to deny it. Only the Christian worldview supplies the preconditions necessary for logic, science, moral standards, and mathematics.

The intelligibility of human experience requires the God of the Bible. Christianity is the only worldview that provides human reason an unchanging foundation for knowledge. All non-Christian systems of thought fail to furnish a foundation for the law of non-contradiction. Thus they cannot provide the footing for knowledge and can offer only an antithetical and incongruous worldview. Unless you believe in God's revealed word, you cannot account for anything in the universe. God is the underlying and infinite ground for all knowledge, proof, evidence, and logic. It is impossible for God not to exist. He is the precondition for all knowledge since knowledge requires the use of the laws of logic. The omniscient, nonmaterial, and unchanging God alone provides the necessary preconditions for the use of nonmaterial, universal, and unchanging laws of logic. To argue at all, you must presuppose that the true God lives; you must use logic. Non-believing thought cannot supply the necessary preconditions for the laws of logic, thus they fall into futility because of the internal contradictions in which they are entangled. Thus the contrary of Christianity is impossible, absurd, and self-refuting, of its own assumptions. Without the Triune God, there could not be knowledge and nothing could make sense.

Plato (who posited realms of being distinct from becoming); Kant (who posited realms of phenomena—or objects perceivable by the mind—distinct from noumena—or objects independent of the mind); and Einstein (who posited realms of the material distinct from the abstract) knew that there is a gulf that separates the material world of hard, concrete objects and the abstract world of ideas, logic, and mathematics. These brilliant men tried to understand the distinction between the material world of physical objects and the nonmaterial world of ideas, concepts, and forms. This gulf between these two worlds demonstrates the impossibility of atheism. Atheism collapses on itself when it declares that only material objects exist: There is no way possible for material objects to transform into nonmaterial ideas. A nonmaterial intelligence is needed to be the transcendent author of the realm of concepts. If human beings consisted only of hard biomass, it would be impossible for them to discern it.

Imagine that you went to the Horseshoe Casino (notice the word "sin" in the middle of the word "casino") in downtown Las Vegas and put a new quarter in the poker machine. The machine rejects your quarter. You look at your coin and it is the real deal; the U.S. Mint has stamped it and it is a good quarter. The poker machine identifies your quarter as a slug. You reject the machine as defective because of the impossibility of the contrary. You go to another poker machine, and according to it your new quarter is legal tender. Thus this new poker machine is correct and the first one was wrong. It is impossible and unthinkable for the first poker machine to have been correct. You have validated the second machine using the argument of the impossibility of the contrary. You have proven the first machine was incorrect and broken. The U.S. Mint transcends the poker machines; you know which poker machine works because of the impossibility of the contrary. Similarly God has "minted" His word and His way in the world. And it is impossible for Him not to exist. If you claim that God does not exist, you must use His minted world—including logic and your senses—to attempt to prove it; because such an attempt would be impossible, God must exist.

The Crowd Can Be Wrong

People usually never think about their intellectual starting points and presuppositions; they just adopt whatever convictions their peers hold to, or whatever the crowd believes. A man walked into his doctor's waiting room and noticed that everyone had stripped down to his underwear. So he took off his shirt and pants and stripped down to his long johns. Another man on another day entered an elevator. It seemed to him as though all the other riders were confused, because they all stood facing the back wall and not the door. So he turned around and joined them in facing the back wall. These two episodes were shown on the TV series *Candid Camera*. The pranks demonstrated how most people will follow the crowd however ridiculous its behavior. Much of the crowd today believes in evolution and many reject the truth of God's word. The majority of these people do so because of their willingness to conform, to forget to think critically. The next few chapters are written to help the reader develop critical thinking skills.

Notes

[1] Carl Sagan, *Contact* (New York: Simon & Schuster, 1985), p. 251.

[2] Cornelius Van Til, *The Defense of Faith* (Phillipsburg, NJ: P & R, 1955), p. 152.

[3] Greg Bahnsen, *Van Til's Apologetic* (Phillipsburg, NJ: P & R, 1998), pp. 479-480.

CHAPTER FIVE

EVOLUTION:
A HOAX AND A FAIRY TALE

Men who believe in any personal or living agency in nature superior to our own are in possession of the one essential element of all religion.[1]

Natural selection is absurdly inadequate to explain the existence of conscious, reflecting, equation solving and poetry writing minds.[2]

The scientific method has no power to resolve disputes about value or teleology. Moreover, when it is trying to describe events in the remote past, such as the origin of life, or complex matters like human behavior, science has to rely on philosophical presuppositions.[3]

It is difficult even to attach a precise meaning to the term "scientific truth." Scientific research can reduce superstition by encouraging people to think and survey things in the terms of cause and effect. Certain it is, akin to a religious feeling, of the rationality or intelligibility of the world lies behind all scientific work of a higher order.[4]

A panel of scholars in 2005 was asked to rank the ten most harmful books. Eight of the ten books they chose, from Marx to Mao, were inspired by Charles Darwin—and yet the panel did not list Darwin's own *The Origin of the Species*. Darwin's theory of evolution helped spawn the greatest crimes in human history. His books, next to the Koran, should be listed as the most harmful ever written. Evolution is an evil and wicked notion that has helped promote the world's greatest atrocities. It is a false theory and a self-refuting ideology.

Evolution is just a theory, just an ideology. The Bible alone declares what is true. Even the atheist Isaac Asimov, the popular science fiction author, admitted in a moment of weakness that "The creation tale in Genesis is very impressive, even in modern terms." Most scientists believe that a Big Bang triggered the birth of the Cosmos. I would ask: If a Big Bang started the universe, who pulled the trigger? Alfred Noyes rightly said: "The universe is centered on neither the earth nor the sun." It is centered on God. Yet according to devoted Darwinian Michael Ruse, evolution is a religion. It has never been and never will be a proven fact. Macro-evolution (the notion that one species can transform into another species) is a hoax, a philosophical swindle, and a wicked fallacy. This chimera has hoodwinked, cheated, and duped more people than any vain philosophy in history. Evolution is false. The universe could not have begun by an unguided big bang. If you watch a grenade explode, you will notice that the pieces do not move in mathematical alignments or orbits. The pieces travel in different and non-ordered directions. An explosion results in chaos, not order. Evolution is the champion delusion, hoax, and fallacy of our time. This swindle of the ages has influenced many fields of science, but it is not long for this world or any other. The theory self-destructs even under surface-level examination. Technological advances in all fields of science have become the evolutionist's foe, not his comrade. Blind chance acting on matter cannot explain the machine-like complexity and efficiency of one cell, cannot explain how the cell is programmed, or where the information in the DNA code came from.

A Code Requires A Code-giver

Lo, heaven and earth exist: they cry out that they have been created....[S]elf-evident is the voice with which these things speak. You, therefore, O Lord, who are beautiful, made these things.[5]

If you eliminate the idea of divine purpose, you have no other logical alternative than to believe that the universe we know has developed by accident. On this principle, all our thinking which traces events back to the intentions or purposes is invalidated. Ever since science began we have been wrong to ask "Why this?" and "Why that?" If "Why?" seeks to uncover an intention, a purpose,...there is ultimately no intention, no purpose.[6]

All living organisms have a DNA code; it is a code that requires information. Information requires a mind, and all living cells have information encoded in them. If I walked down the beach and saw written in the sand: "I love George, now and forever," I would know an intelligent source wrote the sentence. An intelligence was needed to put the information on the sand, just as the DNA code requires an intelligence to encode it into every living cell. So it is blind faith that asserts that the information in a cell comes from blind chance. Chance producing life and information is one of the articles of faith within the evolutionary theory. Theists see design in nature and say there is at least one designer; they see information and know an intelligence put it there; they see machines running efficiently and say there was an intelligence that built them. These conclusions are common sense. Many dictionaries define "stupid" as failing to utilize common sense. A person who asserts materialism or evolution in the face of all these facts is not being intelligent. But facts are not the thrust of apologetics. The true and living God does live; it is impossible for anything else to be true without Him. We are not to trade factual blow with factual blow in our verbal exchange with the evolutionist. We should take the knife from his hand, disarm him, and show him that the sword we hold—the Bible—is the precondition for the intelligibility of our world.

> The conception of [God's] counsel as controlling all things in the universe is the only presupposition which can account for the uniformity of nature which the scientist needs. But the best and only possible proof for God is that his existence is required for the uniformity of nature and for the coherence of all things in the world.[7]

The evolution of the species is a metaphysical claim disseminated by those who believe they are composed of just an assembly of atoms. But how could a mere assembly of physical atoms produce a metaphysical theory? The theory of evolution is religious, and it takes stone-blind faith to believe in it. Materialist evolutionists are fundamentalists.

A Frog to a Prince Without a Kiss

Darwinians believe in a fairy tale. Their fairy tale began once upon a time billions of years ago. One small primal germ fitted and engineered itself together; it liked what it saw in the mirror and decided to reproduce itself. From the primordial soup and this seminal spore, all living organisms evolved. Archaic bacteria decided to move up the ladder, grab life in all its gusto, and evolve into a mushroom. After a million years, the mushroom discovers that being a mushroom is not all it is cracked up to be and that being a spore is highly overrated. So it gathers all its resolve; musters up all its determination; and with its own innate force, after millions and millions of years, evolves into a tadpole. Then the tadpole gets bored and marshals enough resolve to evolve into a fish. After a great period of time, the fish—because it gets sea sick— decides to evolve into a reptile, to experience how sand feels between its toes. The fairy tale goes on to weave its tale, and the reptile evolves into a bird. Then the feathery creature develops a phobia of flying, so it grunts and groans, and after many centuries evolves into a mammal. The mammal evolves into an ape, and the ape decides it likes poetry, music, and football, so it decides to become a man. In this fairy tale of evolution, instead of a princess kissing a frog and the frog becoming a prince, the frog evolves into a prince without needing a kiss. It takes blind faith to believe in such a mythology. In the beginning God created the heavens and the earth: Without this belief as an assumed starting point, nothing makes sense, and we fall for delusions as silly as pixie-tales.

It is not just difficult to believe that the universe can produce everything from stardust to Da Vinci, germs to Beethoven, tadpoles to Shakespeare, and the primordial soup to Michael Jordan's slam dunks; it is not just straining credulity to believe that we are turbocharged apes: It is impossible for these things to be true. The problem with evolution is not just Herbert Spencer's "unknowable mystery." It is impossible for materialism and evolution to account for morality, reason, and mathematics. The nineteenth century scientist and philosopher Thomas Henry Huxley ranted that we all came from a "murky pale of protoplasm." Not only is Huxley stuck in the mire of mere assertion, but his statement—like all others based on materialism—is self-stultifying and self-defeating. It is destroyed on its own terms. If we are the result only of a material process of matter and motion, the evolutionist could not justify the nonmaterial logic he uses in forming his arguments. If he is correct and there is nothing beyond the material realm, then his theory is the byproduct of a material, biological process alone and cannot be trusted. The evolutionist cannot account for his use of reason. Thus to employ reason to propagate the theory of evolution is to refute oneself.

Bacteria Are the Fittest

There are no grounds in science or logic for a bacterium to evolve into a "higher" form. Bacteria are the fittest creatures on the planet, rivaled only by cockroaches. These two types of organisms do not need to evolve; they survive quite nicely. Nothing is more tenacious, more resilient, stouter, more productive and self-procuring than bacteria. Why would they need to evolve? Why would cockroaches need to evolve? They could survive a nuclear bomb. The organisms that evolutionists claim as the "higher" creatures die off easier and more quickly and produce far fewer offspring. The higher up the ladder, the more likely the organism is to become extinct or be put on the endangered species list.

Look how fragile the whales and the great apes are. Creatures with a large body mass are much less fit than bacteria and cockroaches. Evolutionists do not have to worry about merely a missing link; the whole chain is gone. Only God and His revelation can give us a foundation for science. The theory of the survival of the fittest does not comport with the reality of bacteria and cockroaches; they do not need to evolve into higher forms; they do just fine without knowing about Mickey Mouse or Plato. Bacteria would not become stouter and produce more survivable offspring if they could read poetry or applaud Tiger Woods. Bacteria do not have determination or conviction; even if they had resolve, how could it give them the innate force to evolve? They would need purpose and the means to fulfill it—a teleological reason that could only come with intelligence and purpose. A universe consisting only of material things could not produce teleology; hence evolution is a myth, a fable for profligate adults; it not only does not comport with the facts, it is impossible—because in the beginning God created the heavens and the earth.

Odds, Probability, and Certainty

Sir Fred Hoyle, the Cambridge astronomer, once said that the odds of life arising by chance are about as high as "a tornado blowing through a junk yard and forming a Boeing 747."[8] The analogy is devastating to those who submit to the blind faith of evolution. Yet it is much worse than that. There are no odds for the existence of God, no probabilities. It is impossible for the God of the Bible not to exist. Without God one could not discuss or argue about the theory of evolution. The Search for Extraterrestrial Intelligence (S.E.T.I.) scans the heavens for codes, information, language, and patterns. These researchers base their work on the theory that finding a radio signal with a code would prove there are intelligent beings in the vast reaches of the universe. The premise is: A code presupposes a code-giver. A code-giver has intelligence; within the Christian worldview that makes sense. The baffling thing is to watch the scientists, who study the DNA code, fail to make the same deduction they would if an alien sent a simple code over the air waves. A code-giver presupposes an intelligence—a fact often ignored by scientists. Fuzzy reasoning is the primary problem with the theory of evolution.

Unbelieving men suppress the truth in unrighteousness. Without the one true God as the pre-requirement of all thought, one could not make sense of anything. My uncle is not a monkey, and my grandfather is not a polliwog. I am not a product of monkeydom; I am created in the image of God. Mozart, Milton, and moms are not the mere products of animated stardust. Evolutionists want their father to be a muskrat and their mother to be an opossum. They delight in the fairy tale that their great aunt was a tadpole or snapping turtle. But if man evolved from animals, then all humans are animals, and they have license to behave like animals. Strangely enough, the doctrine of evolution presupposes God, since it employs logic and reason in arguing its theory. Science presupposes God. Induction presupposes God. All the skeptics' absurd theories require God. All true and false postulates require God and His revelation as a precondition of intelligibility.

Most arguments against the theory of evolution claim to be probable. Their proponents do not speak of certainty. The Bible speaks of God as the creator with absolute certainty. There is not a cosmic odds-giver crunching the probability of the existence of God Almighty.

A single cell is made up of 100,000 molecules; 10,000 finely tuned, interrelated chemical reactions occur simultaneously; and a cell contains in its nucleus a digitally coded database larger than thirty volumes of an encyclopedia. The odds that so intricate a thing would come about by chance are so overwhelming as to be a mathematical impossibility. The truth of the matter is that God's existence is not a probability. The odds-giver should not give a thousand to one odds that this world was created by a creator. There is absolute certainty that God lives and that He created all things in the heavens and the earth—period. We must have God as a condition for the created universe or nothing in it would make sense.

> The wicked in his proud countenance does not seek God; God is in none of his thoughts....[Y]our judgments are far above, out of his sight....He has said in his heart, I shall not be moved; I shall never be in adversity (Psalms 10:4-6).

Blind Chance or Design?

Sir Fred Hoyle discredits evolution by pointing out that "The laws of nuclear physics have been deliberately designed with regard to the consequences they produce inside stars. If this is so, apparently random quirks have become part of a deep-laid scheme." He called creation a "put up job." We have certainty that God designed the universe. The Lord declared that He did, and without Him we cannot justify science. We know that God lives and that He designed and created all things; that is not just probably true, it has to be true. Those who affirm the Christian worldview delight in the "evidence" of God's creation. His fingerprints are on every part of the universe from the smallest atom to the largest galaxy. I enjoy examining the proof of God's design and engineering. But within my worldview, everything is evidence of God having created time, space, and matter. There is nothing in the world that is not evidence for a creator when I affirm Biblical presuppositions. It is impossible for God not to be the creator. We have a perfect certainty that God hurled and fashioned this universe together for His glory. We must stand on God's word and say to the world: God lives, and He is not silent. There is no doubt that He lives, due to the fact that doubt presupposes the Triune God. All doubts depend on logic, reason, and morality, and all those elements presuppose God.

In the beginning God created the heavens and the earth (Genesis 1:1).

I rejoice when I discover that if the earth were 10% larger or 10% smaller, life would be impossible. The earth is tilted at just the correct angle and has just the right mixture of gas in its atmosphere; the moon is just the right size at just the right distance; and the earth is at just the right distance from the sun to sustain life. No other known planet is organized with such precision to ensure that life can survive on it. This evidence will convince all believers. These are very happy facts, but not uninterpreted or brute facts; a skeptic could dismiss and explain them away. The facts do not explain themselves. But the cool skeptic does not care. He holds to a different worldview and believes in different presuppositions. The battle is not over facts; it is over worldviews and the foundational assumption by which we interpret facts.

The fossil record has not produced birds with one-half or one-quarter wings. What use would a halfway-evolved wing be in the struggle for survival? The nonfunctioning appendage would get in the way and inhibit survival, not enhance it. We do not find fish with one-half or one-third fins, because these would not assist in the survival of the species. The extra weight and frozen body part would hinder its survival. Body parts not fully formed (incomplete lungs, warm-blooded hearts, partial eyes, etc.) would be a hindrance to any organism trying to survive. And when did the fish or the birds get together and decide to grow wings and fins? "Hey, Hal I'm bored, let's do something different tonight and grow some quarter wings, so our future ancestors will grow full wings and be able to fly in a few million years." That sounds ridiculous, and it is; it involves teleology, or striving for a goal; and that is the reason it sounds so preposterous. Unanimated matter and animals, void of reason, cannot decide to embrace teleology. Yet the skeptic will still invent fanciful theories to explain how animals evolved wings and fins. The main problem with evolution is that, without God, one cannot account for facts of any kind.

The heavens declare the glory of God; and the firmament shows His handiwork (Psalms 19:1).

Information Presupposes Intelligence

We have been taught in public school that all our cells contain DNA. DNA is in every cell of every living thing. We are fascinated by the knowledge that DNA works in a partnership with RNA. DNA is a code that sends off a message. Any time we see messages or information in our world, we assume that an intelligent being placed it there. If we go to Maui, take a long stroll through the jungle, and observe writing on a tree trunk that says "Joe loves Lori now and forever," we know that the wind, acting upon some stick, did not write those words by chance. Why? Because there is information in the writing on the tree. The precondition for information is intelligence. DNA is a readable code; intelligent design is a precondition for living things. Many psuedo-scientists are pointing microphones into graveyards and "haunted houses," hoping to hear from intelligent beings in another dimension. What are they looking for? They are searching for language and a code. But an intelligent, otherworldly being—God—has already contacted mankind. He has written a code and a message in all our cells, declaring that He lives. Most important of all, He has revealed His person and His way in the Bible. It takes a person gifted in self-deception to conclude that the information in every cell on the planet came by chance. Nowhere else do we find information, codes, or messages coming by chance. When you read the plethora of articles on cloning or gene therapy, notice how often they use words like book, map, code, tissue engineering, design, patterns, message, blueprint, reading, deciphering, and many others which presuppose intelligence; such words are devastating to the atheist. An intelligent God designed us and implanted the DNA blueprint in all living creatures.

Every cell in every living thing has a digitally coded database that is more voluminous in information content than a large stack of biology books. The intelligible information stored in one molecule of DNA would fill a stack of books from the earth to the moon. This information is encoded in DNA and RNA by numerous enzymes. These active proteins are capable of reading, deciphering, and communicating. All these different parts and mechanisms must be set up independently and simultaneously, or the individual part would not be of any use. All these varied mechanisms must be independently and precisely set up, wired, and installed at the same time. The odds of all these different, intelligent, machine-like processes evolving by chance, simultaneously and with precision and complete compatibility, are unthinkable.

Poems, written advertisements, and DNA all have "specified complexity" and a high information content. High-information content demands an intelligence behind it. All living cells have DNA and a set of chemical instructions written with amino acids and proteins. Suppose you stumbled upon a pile of rocks on a mountainside, placed in a formation that spelled-out: "Go USC!" You would know that rain water beating on the rocks, mixed with air-bombed bird poop that dropped on the dirt, could not have written this message. You would recognize that an intelligent being wrote it—, maybe a hiker, or perhaps a Trojan fan. Similarly, DNA must have an intelligent being as its author, since it contains complex and specific information that could not come from chance plus time acting on matter. Maybe an alien, a pantheon of gods or Hume's big vegetable wrote these biological missives in all cells. The information theory, outside the Christian worldview, cannot prove the Biblical God, but within the Christian worldview it is a powerful "proof."

Evolution Is Impossible

Evolution is indeed impossible; it is not just implausible. Biologically sturdy ants would not need to evolve into the top-ten list of endangered species like the great apes. A stout rat would not evolve into a fragile wolf or giraffe. A strong and resilient bacterium would not evolve into a weak and quickly extinct Dodo bird. The so-called lower species are usually the strongest and most fit to survive. If reproducing the strongest and greatest number of offspring is the means to preserve a species, then the ant and the rat are among the "highest" species. The following "facts" make evolution impossible. Living amino acids are in a different form than nonliving amino acids; they do not switch over into nonliving amino acids in non-biological systems. Living molecules could not have formed without an oxygen-rich atmosphere, yet oxygen eats up the pre-protein-chained amino acids. Without oxygen, a living organism could not live; there would be an absence of a life-demanding ozone layer. Furthermore, a pre-biotic cell would be destroyed in an oxygen-rich environment before it could evolve into a living cell by the oxygen itself. Thus oxygen is mandatory for life, though it kills off the pre-life before it can live.

Many modern scientists have discovered that every cell in every living organism has many interrelated, interconnected, and inter-depended parts. These bio-pieces could not have evolved simultaneously to produce immediately functioning mini-machines in living cells. Michael Behe uses a mousetrap to illustrate the problem of "irreducibly complex" biological systems. For the mouse trap to work, it needs many parts in the system to function at the same time. The catch, the spring, the holding bar, the hammer, and the platform all have to function simultaneously. A living cell has many different systems with dozens of parts. No biological system could work unless all its parts functioned simultaneously. Thus there is no chance that a biological organ could go through many, slight and successive modifications, as required by the theory of evolution. The idea that all these parts within the organ evolved into a perfect fit simultaneously is mere fancy. Darwinian evolution is impossible, and the very theory of macro-evolution presupposes God. Logic is a precondition for any theory, including a fallacious theory like Darwinism.

Questions for the Evolutionist

The following is a list of a few simple questions that I have found stump evolutionists.

Where in the fossil record are the transitional forms between invertebrate organisms and vertebrate organisms?

How did the human eye, capable of performing ten billion calculations per second, evolve by chance?

How do lifeless chemicals come alive?

What is the evolutionary advantage of an organism having a half-wing on its way to a full wing? Would not the extra weight of the half-wing and the potential clumsiness of the useless appendage lower the chance of survival rather than enhance it?

Does a worm, with a mutation that causes a leg to evolve, increase its survivability? Would not the new leg reduce its chance for survival?

How did warm-blooded birds evolve from cold-blooded reptiles?

Does the doctrine of the survival of the fittest assert that the organisms that produce the greatest number of surviving offspring are the most fit? If so, why would a cockroach or bacterium ever ascend and eventually evolve into large body-mass organisms that are extremely susceptible to extinction and produce much fewer offspring? Do bugs and bacteria *need* to evolve?

Can information such as the DNA code come from a non-intelligence? Is there anywhere where we observe a non-intelligent process producing information?

Can chance plus time plus agitation produce information? (Try putting a pen and paper in your clothes dryer and turn it on high heat; even after a hundred loads, you don't get Milton).

How can chance plus energy plus time produce the "bristling high-tech machinery" of the living cell? These tiny living machines are fitted with active sensors, gates, pumps, and labeled markers. Can all this automated biological machinery, equipped with power plants, automated bio-factories, and recycling centers, all be produced by blind chance?

Is it because science cannot supply the conditions for morality that it is prone to fakes, forgeries, and frauds? Many of these frauds have been exposed in medical and scientific studies. The investigators discovered that the dishonest scientists were seeking grant money, which motivated them to lie about their medical research. This dishonest research for testing medical treatments, the Piltdown man hoax, and other projects, is harmful. In January 2000, the Archaeoraptor was touted by the *National Geographic* magazine as a bird and later was found to be a fake! Why is there such a long history of scientific hoaxes and fraud?

Deny God and affirm evolutionary materialism and you undermine morality. Nature offers endless scores of "inhumane" conduct. Are humans to follow the animals that kidnap and force females to have sex with them? Should we act like praying mantises and black widows that devour their mates? One finds a plethora of beastly killings, forced intercourse, and voids of egalitarianism in nature. Monogamy, self-sacrifice, and enduring love are missing in most of the animal kingdom. Without God, there is no reason mankind should not practice the same brutality.

The Brain Thing

The materialist atheist asserts that the mind is the physical brain. There are no nonphysical actions taking place in the human brain. But if the human mind consisted only of hard chemicals and neurons bouncing around in the skull, human thoughts would be no more true or valued than an afternoon tamale food belch; both would be just chemical reactions. Thus there is no rational reason to consider my thoughts more important than a burp; they are just meaningless and empty chemical reactions. That idea is, of course, self-contradictory. If your thoughts and words are meaningless, then they are not true; hence, your thoughts cannot be meaningless. Your thoughts are not just concrete chemical reactions.

A mind, distinct from the brain, destroys the theory of evolution. Evolutionary materialists do not believe mankind has a spirit. The soul is only "a little wind and smoke," in the words of the Christian philosopher Blaise Pascal. Research on the brain can lead to the conclusion that the mind is independent of the brain. Some legitimate science has uncovered reasons to believe that life survives physical death. A Yale University professor (using scientific theory alone) wrote that he would "bet yes" that the afterlife is a fact. When one submits to God's revelation, there is no betting. It is impossible for God and the afterlife He reveals not to exist. To ask a question about a possible afterlife presupposes that God lives and that His word is true. When the atheist backs up in a conversation and says, "Hold on, I'm searching for a word," point out the inconsistency. We should ask them: "Who's searching?" Those who claim that only the physical world exists and that their mind is just a block of flesh cannot answer that question. Frequently, they will see their dilemma. Huxley, in one of his moments of weakness, asked, "How is it that anything so remarkable as the state of consciousness comes about as a result of irritating nervous tissue? Is it just as unaccountable as the appearance of the genie, when Aladdin rubbed his lamp?"

Research has demonstrated that there is a distinction between the mind and the brain. In one study, brain surgeons opened patients' skulls to expose their brains. The researchers then electrically stimulated the area of the brain which lifts the right arm. The patients' arms lifted without their permission. Then the scientists instructed their patients to resist the lifting of the arm when they stimulated the same spot. This time all the patients could resist. The experiment proved that the mind can control the brain. Another study, conducted by U.C.L.A., had doctors give depressed patients two sets of pills. One was an antidepressant medicine and the other was a placebo. Both groups said they experienced a relief of symptoms: 52% of those who received the medication, and 38% of those who received the placebo. The interesting thing was the discovery that the brain waves of the placebo-taking patients acutely changed after taking the fake pill. Their brain chemistry and brain waves were altered without any medication, merely from their own "minds." The mind controls the brain and can change it; the mind is distinct from the brain. The researchers reported that they were "stunned," because there were actual "hardware" changes in the brain by the power of suggestion. The mind can change and alter how the brain works. These experiments are clear evidence that the mind moves the brain and is distinct from the brain tissue. Evidence is good, but remember that evidence can be interpreted in immoral ways.

Rocks and Dogs Appreciating Art?

Without presupposing the God of the Bible, one cannot account for any theory, even the theory of evolution. One cannot supply the necessary preconditions for the use of logic and reason without God. The materialist proclaims that only material objects exist, so he cannot account for the nonmaterial logic that he puts into service in forging his theory. He uses logic, but he cannot account for it. The nonbeliever must steal from the Christian worldview to make any pronouncement about any object or any concept in the world. One cannot even account for science without the Christian worldview. Pastor T. Dewitt Talmage wittingly said, "Science and scripture are the bass and soprano of the same tune." He likened the skeptic Robert Ingersoll's attack on the Bible as to "a grasshopper on a railway line when the express comes thundering along." He also quipped that "science is a boy and revelation is a man." He was demonstrating that revelation is more mature and reliable than science. We could go beyond that conclusion and say that, without a man—a father—a boy could not exist. One cannot have science without God. The God of the Bible is the precondition for science. Science uses induction, empirical testing, logic, and morality. One cannot account for any of those dynamics without God and His revelation.

The atheistic worldview proposes that mankind, with all his skyscrapers, supersonic jets, operas, art, and literature, is merely a more complex block of whirling subatomic particles than rocks, carrots, and squirrels. An atheist can use science, but he can never account for it without God. God and His revelation are the foundations for science. The Christian is not to be a concordist—one who attempts to find agreement or concord between revelation and science. The truth of God is the precondition for true science. Science needs God and His revelation. God does not need science.

Anything But God: The False God of Chance

Blind chance acting on matter cannot explain anything, including itself. If you spill your beer by accident, you do not ask the beer how it got there. The beer is an accident and cannot explain itself. The Bud isn't "wiser." One needs a person to explain the beer spill. If our world is an accident, just some cosmic burp, then we cannot explain ourselves, including the statement that we cannot explain ourselves; this is one of those self-refuting statements that destroy atheism. These statements, if true, are false (see Chapter Six for more on self-refuting statements). Thus the proposition that we are an accident that cannot explain itself is a false statement; it is self-demolishing. As you read through this book, you will notice, in the dialogues and commentary, that everything not based on the Christian worldview is false. Nothing true that an atheist can assert will contradict Christianity. The God of the Bible has all the answers, and without God no one would have an answer to any question. Jesus announced that He was "the truth." He is the truth, and the Holy Spirit is the Spirit of truth. To make any consistent and true statement, one must base it on the God of truth. Anything written or spoken that attempts to contradict and overturn the Lord's revelation is self-defeating and fallacious. We know that we are not just a random accident produced from a primordial and impersonal Big Bang. An explosion does not have order. The universe does have order, thus we are no accident. We call living things organisms. An *organism* presupposes *organization* and structure. Who organized the organisms? We cannot be the product of self-organizing stardust. Without God one could not account for the logic needed in creating the hypothesis.

Mathematician J.W. Sullivan described evolution as "an article of faith." When I believed in evolution (and I did "believe"), I was troubled by the fact that in the fossil record one-half giraffe's necks were never found. I shook my head in bewilderment when I mused on the fact that only a fully developed eye would help an organism survive. A third of an eye and a three-quarters of an eye would hinder the fitness and the survivability of an organism. The DNA code also bothered me. If one saw a neon sign flashing "Loosest Slots on Jupiter," one would assume intelligence designed the sign and put the information on it. The information would not have gotten there by chance. Could the non-intelligent process of chance really create the universe by some cosmic explosion? Could life come from non-life? Could intelligence come from non-intelligence? Could slime evolve to ponder the divine? Could a frog evolve into a prince? Rocks and cats do not appreciate Rembrandt; why do I? These questions that bounced around in my non-Christian head made sleeping at night difficult. I usually had to have loud music blaring so I would not ponder these refutations of my faith in evolution.

The Self-refuting Nature of Naturalism

By the word of the LORD the heavens were made; and all the host of them by the breath of His mouth....For He spoke, and it was done; He commanded, and it stood fast (Psalms 33:6, 9).

Refuting evolution is easy. The evolutionists live and testify on blind faith. They tell us — as Richard Dawkins does in *The Blind Watchmaker* — that living things "give the appearance of having been designed for a purpose." It is easy to refute such nonsense with compelling evidential arguments. But one must not exchange evidence with the evolutionist and then believe that the one who is the best lawyer wins the argument. The evolutionist's objections to Christianity are to be answered in the same way one answers all objections. It is easy to uproot the foundations of evolution and demonstrate that only Christianity can give a foundation for science and knowledge. Evolution is a faith-based system and cannot account for or justify the use of induction, logic, and morality.

Evolutionists have a pre-commitment to "metaphysical naturalism," a religious and philosophical system that asserts the universe and everything in it are made up solely of matter and motion. Skeptics assume that only the material world exists. That is why Dawkins begins *The Blind Watchmaker* with this confession: "Biology is the study of complicated things that give the appearance of having been designed for a purpose." Dawkins then attempts, in the remainder of the book, to refute this observation, and does so without even blushing. Such inconsistency lies behind the theories of Dawkins and all evolutionists who attempt to marshal empirical facts to support their non-empirical theories that insist living organisms only *appear* to be designed. Theories like this demonstrate the bias of the evolutionist's foundational pre-commitments and clearly show that materialism is the presupposition behind them.

The biggest problem for the evolutionary theory is that it is a theory. By definition, a theory is not a material object but is abstract and nonphysical. The evolutionist posits the idea that only the material world exists, all the time asserting an idea that is nonmaterial. An idea, a theory, and a hypothesis are not material objects; they are nonmaterial. The evolutionist uses a nonmaterial theory to assert that it is only possible for the material cosmos to exist. One can discern with just a superficial examination of the materialist's claims that such a theory is self-nullifying; it commits philosophical suicide. The theories of the anti-theists are exposed inasmuch as they are self-contradicting and self-terminating.

David Hume, the eighteenth century empiricist and skeptic, said, "[Of a]ny volume...let us ask, does it contain any abstract reasoning concerning quantity or number? No. Does it contain any experimental reasoning concerning matter of fact and existence? No. Commit it to the flames; for it can contain nothing but sophistry and illusion." Hume makes a self-refuting blunder here. His own statement must be thrown to the flames, because it lacks any "reasoning concerning quantity and number," as well as "any experimental reasoning concerning a matter of fact or existence."

A Complete Theory

If we should discover a complete theory...we shall...be able to take part in the question of why it is that we and the Universe exist. If we find the answer to that it will be the ultimate triumph of human reason—for then we would know the mind of God.[9]

Carl Sagan looked up at the stars, set against the velvet of the night, and declared that only the cosmos exists. He assumed omniscience in this boast—a fanciful boast that could never be verified. As Sagan matured, he seemed to sober up to the reality that the universe and living organisms exhibit order, complexity, and design. So he plunged, with eyes wide shut, farther into the aphotic folly, proposing that the design might have come from alien life forms seeding our globe. He reduced the human race to an extraterrestrial science project and revealed his bias against theism. Sagan's speculations required blind faith to believe. There is no empirical evidence for extraterrestrials. Unlike God, they are not the precondition for the intelligibility of the cosmos.

Our argumentation should end up by showing that the unbeliever's presuppositions (worldview) would consistently lead to foolishness and the destruction of knowledge.[10]

No school of science has ever frightened theists as much as geology. Many geologists proclaim that the strata of the earth contradict the Bible. But, as discovered by Steve Austin in his study of layered strata formed by the eruption of Mount St. Helen's, there is no disagreement between geological facts and the Bible. Many scientists may expose alleged Biblical contradictions, but they are only contradictions if one begins with faulty presuppositions.

Professor Steven A. Austin, of the Institute of Creation Research, has demonstrated that layered strata could be formed in an instant by volcanic activity like the Mount St. Helen's eruption in the 1980's. Either way, the "facts" do not speak for themselves. All facts must be interpreted through the eyes of philosophical presuppositions.

God has spoken: With this presupposition, you can justify reality and your investigation of reality. When you base your worldview on God and His word, you can justify science, induction, the evaluation of evidence, and your use of reason. The nonbeliever cannot justify one item in all reality and cannot provide the necessary preconditions for the investigation of reality. Thus the nonbeliever cannot account for geology and science. How do you know that induction is true? How do you know, when you test something and get the same result a thousand times, that you will get the same result the next time? The materialist does not know. If I put my hand in the fire, I will get burned: Why can I depend on that the next time? The Christian can depend on it because God's revelation has told him that induction is true and he can count on it. The nonbeliever cannot justify induction; he uses it and takes it for granted, yet cannot account for it—it just is.

The non-Christian has to live by blind faith. The Christian worldview is the precondition for science. We do not need to try to get scientific approval for the Bible. Science needs approval from God's word. Charles Spurgeon, in his book *The Greatest Fight in the World Rightly Maintained,* writes: "If scientists agree to our believing part of the Bible...their assent is of no more consequence to our faith than...the consent of the mole to the eagle's sight." We do not need the affirmation of scientists; they need the affirmation of God's revelation. Without scripture, the scientists cannot provide the rational preconditions needed for science.

Many have a pre-commitment to materialism, yet they cannot justify that commitment. Justifying anything transcends materialism, because justifications are not material objects. If materialism is valid, we could get as much truth from the purring motor of a Chevy as from the motor of human cognition. However, we do not observe journalists waiting to interview race car motors after a race; they always seem to interview the driver, who has a mind. A mind is more than just a machine. There is a "ghost in the machine"—the human spirit—that helps make up a soul.

A Talk with An Average Joe

I have had the opportunity to discuss the myth of Darwinian

evolution with a number of people from all walks of life. Here is one such conversation with Joe:

Mike: Hey, I noticed your car has a Darwin fish on it. Do you believe in evolution?

Joe: Of course. Are you one of those fundamentalists who are stuck in the tenth century?

Mike: That's quite a question. Actually, I like to discuss the theory of evolution with people who hold that position and pray that they repent and trust in Christ. Have you studied the science of DNA?

Joe: Yes, I have. It provides great evidence for the evolutionary process. Human DNA is almost 98% identical to ape DNA. This is strong evidence.

Mike: Does DNA have a code and information content in it?

Joe: Yes, that's one of its main functions.

Mike: Have you ever seen information come from anything but an intelligent being?

Joe: Well, uh, no.

Mike: Information requires intelligence. If I heard someone tapping on the other side of a wall in a language such as the Morse code and it spelled out, "Help me, I've been kidnapped by a circus clown with bad breath," I would assume that there is an intelligent being behind the wall in need of help. The reason I would know that there must be a person behind the tapping is that it came in the form of a code, not just the random tapping of a bird or a machine. The code requires intelligence, and biologists call it the DNA code. Code! Can you explain where, unless an intelligent being wrote it in the cells, the DNA code came from?

Joe: Well, I've never thought about it that way.

Mike: I never did either until I started learning to think in a critical manner. I'd encourage you to turn from your ways and trust in Jesus Christ. You and I have sinned. We've broken God's law by lying, stealing, hating, missing church, lusting, and many other sins. Jesus died to remove all the sins of His people.

Here's a tract with an invitation to our church.
Come by and check it out.

Joe: Thanks.

In the Beginning: God

In the beginning God created...(Genesis 1:1).

The opening verse of the Bible declares that God created the heavens and the earth. God created the universe out of nothing. For many decades, most non-Christian scientists did not believe that the universe had a beginning. Today most scientists believe that the universe did have a starting point, and that is one of the many reasons we are not to submit God's word to modern science. Rather, all science must be submitted to God's word. No ancient philosophy or religion other than the Judeo-Christian religion asserts that the whole universe was created out of nothing at one point in time. The Hindus believe Brahma created the water from an eternal universe. He then moved over the water and out of his eye went the sun, out of his lips went the fire, and out of his ear went the air. Then Brahma got tired and laid down for over four million years. After that little catnap, this Rip Van Winkle of a god destroyed the world and then out of the chaotic material created the world again; he did so again and again. He continues to sleep, wake up, destroy the universe, and then make it again—creation, demolition, then four million years of sleep. Brahma and all the false gods may sleep, but the true and living God neither slumbers nor sleeps (Psalm 121:4). He alone created the whole universe out of nothing at one moment in time. Only the true God supplies a foundation on which to study, analyze, and make theories about the origin of the universe. Only the living God allows us to account for the logic, induction, and ethics required to make scientific discoveries.

The earth is always changing. One cannot vest hope, thought, or philosophy on the earthly. One cannot base his ethics, reason, and nobility on a system of thought built on a physical universe that is in a constant state of flux. A changing cosmos cannot produce unchanging things like the laws of logic. Again, those entities transcend the physical universe. Intellect in submission to God's revealed word is the only means by which to make sense of the universe. Kepler said it best in describing the creation as a "sacred sermon, a veritable hymn to God the Creator."

Without God There Is No Meaning

Existentialists, like the atheist Jean Paul Sartre, claim that life has no meaning. But the assertion of the absence of meaning presupposes meaning. There has to be a standard of meaning even to assert that there is no meaning in life. If one feels isolated in a sea of meaninglessness, one must be isolated from something. The schools of philosophy that promulgate the meaninglessness of all things presuppose meaning, and meaning presupposes the living God. To make a claim that something is not, presupposes something that is. Isolation and meaninglessness presuppose the God of scripture. One cannot escape God through vain philosophy of any stripe. If life is meaninglessness, that would include the theory that life is meaningless. The theory is self-nullifying. Life has meaning. And the claim that life does not have meaning presupposes God. The non-believing existentialist wants to rest in his self-imposed ignorance. As C. S. Lewis said, "Heaven understands hell and hell does not understand heaven." Non-Christians do not want to be stimulated out of their self-deception. The Bible is the philosophical alarm clock. Every existential cynic and iconoclast relies on logic, language, and ethics to propagate his views. The precondition for logic, language, and ethics is God Almighty. The existential escape is no escape. There is no escape from reason, morality, language, or God.

The Inescapable Truth of Christianity

All non-Christian thought, including Darwinism, ultimately destroys the possibility of logic, science, moral codes, and all aspects of human experience. Christianity provides the preconditions for human experience; it is inescapable and is the only worldview that does not make nonsense of the cosmos and human experience. If Christianity is not true, then knowledge is impossible. Christianity is certain and unavoidable; it alone rejects man's autonomy. Human beings are not omniscient or omnipotent; thus humanity cannot account for universals in the laws of logic and mathematics without God. The Christian worldview declares that God has spoken and humanity is not autonomous. With Christianity out of the picture, one affirms autonomy, which leads to self-contradiction. Christianity declares a worldview that supplies a means to understand human experience; it announces that the sovereign God has revealed knowledge of Himself and the cosmos. All non-Christian worldviews, including naturalism, are autonomous and cannot provide the preconditions for the intelligibility of anything in the world because they are non-universal and self-stultifying. All species of thought contrary to Christian theism are arbitrary, self-contradictory, and impossible. Autonomous thought is impossible because it is contradicted on its own assumptions, and hence grabs a shovel and digs its own grave. The Triune God has spoken in Jesus and the Bible. He is the precondition for the intelligibility of all human experience. Without God one must fall into self-contradictions.

Without the Triune God, all reasoning fails; thus there could not be science. There is not a non-Christian view of the creation that can make sense out of reasoning, science, and morality. An atheist scientist cannot account for his use of nonphysical logic in his scientific reasoning. Logic is not physical; it is transcendent, universal, and abstract. Only the Christian world and life view can supply the necessary preconditions for the nonmaterial, unchanging, and universal laws of logic. The laws of logic cannot be found in a beaker or a test-tube. You cannot purchase a set of laws of logic on sale at Target; they are not concrete and physical. Only the transcendent, immutable, universal, and nonphysical God can provide the necessary preconditions for the transcendent, immutable, universal, and nonphysical laws of logic. It is impossible for the atheistic scientist to be correct in declaring that nothing exists except the material. For even that declaration is nonmaterial and hence false. It is impossible for God not to exist.

They are like children sitting in the marketplace, and calling to one another, saying: We played the flute for you, and you did not dance; we mourned, and you did not weep....But wisdom is justified by all her children (Luke 7:32-35).

Notes

[1] The Duke of Argyle, *Reign of Law* (New York: Boies, 1884), p. 269.

[2] Philip Johnson, *Reasoning in the Balance* (Downers Grove, IL: Intervarsity Press, 1995), p. 89.

[3] Ibid., p. 200.

[4] Albert Einstein, *Essays in Science* (New York: Haddon, 1934), p. 11.

[5] Saint Augustine, *Confessions* (Garden City, NY: Doubleday, 1960), p. 280.

[6] Harry Blaimires, *On Christian Truth* (Ann Arbor: Servant Books, 1983), p. 29.

[7] Cornelius Van Til, *The Defense of Faith* (Philadelphia: P & R, 1955), p. 103.

[8] Roy Peacock, *A Brief History of Eternity* (Wheaton, IL: Crossway Books, 1990), p. 145.

[9] Ibid., p. 120.

[10] Greg Bahnsen, *Answering Objections, Biblical Worldview* (VII; Feb., 1991), Covenant Media Foundation, p. 1.

CHAPTER SIX

WHAT'S TRUE FOR YOU, ISN'T TRUE FOR ME; THAT'S TRUE

Presuppositional apologetics is...a helpful tool....With it we attempt to discover what [people believe] and why they believe it. We can then draw their belief system to its logical conclusions, showing the fallacy of such a system. This is often enlightening to a nonbeliever because many have never thoroughly thought through what they believe. We can contrast their belief system with one based on Biblical truth.[1]

I am beginning to feel that without contradiction and paradox I cannot get anywhere near that truth which will set me free.[2]

O Dear Lord, you are equal to everyone. For you there is no distinction between your sons, friends[,] or enemies.[3]

The law of non-contradiction is the foundation upon which all rationality is established.[4]

Freedom is slavery. Two plus two make five.[5]

Self-refuting Statements

Van Tilian apologist and philosopher John Frame stresses the need to understand presuppositions: "The obedient believer is one who counts the Word of God as the surest truth he knows, as his presupposition.... The unbeliever is one who rejects that presupposition....The commitment of his heart is to oppose God, and so he seeks to escape his responsibility to obey any scriptural law, including the norms of knowledge. But he cannot succeed. Indeed, he cannot even attack the law without assuming its truth, and thus, his thinking is muddled."[6] The prophet Jeremiah pronounced the following: "Your own wickedness will correct you, and your backslidings will rebuke you. Know therefore and see that it is an evil and bitter thing that you have forsaken the LORD your God, and the fear of Me is not in you, says the Lord GOD of hosts" (Jeremiah 2:19).

A self-refuting statement is a universal statement, not based on God's word, that self-destructs and invalidates itself based on its own propositions. If the statement were true, it would be false. A self-refuting statement is self-defeating and self-invalidating; it nullifies itself and cannot be true; if it were true, it would be false.

The Self-deceived Assert Self-refuting Statements

A self-refuting statement fails to satisfy its own premise; it is necessarily false. Nietzsche unwittingly demonstrated this when he wrote this self-refuting statement: "There are many eyes. Thus there are many truths. Hence there is no truth." My question to Nietzsche would be: "Is that true?" If it is, it is false; if it is not, it is false. It cannot be true. People want to be self-deceived and will assert contradictory statements to avoid the truth found in Christ. Skepticism and every non-Christian assertion will always self-destruct. What they attempt to justify confutes itself. If you would be rational, you must be a Christian to account for the preconditions of the intelligibility of reason. We do not have to go around refuting every infidel's errant proposition; they will refute and destroy themselves on their own terms. If a proposition contradicts the Bible, it commits philosophical suicide. There are internal inconsistencies in all non-Christian systems of philosophy and thought. The Christian has total certainty and the unbeliever has total uncertainty. Any notion that is contrary to Biblical thought is false.

The following list of self-refuting propositions is given to demonstrate the gaping defects in all non-Christian thought. Self-nullifying statements fail to satisfy their own premises. They are necessarily false. Below I have listed a number of self-refuting assertions. The self-refuting statement is written first, followed by a stultifying question or appropriate response.

- You can't know anything for sure.
  Are you sure of that?

- You shouldn't judge.
  Is that your judgment?

- You shouldn't push your views on others.
  Are you pushing that view on me?

- There is no certainty.
  Are you certain of that?

- All things are relative.
  Then so is that statement, and thus it is not true and all things are not relative. If a statement is relative, it is not binding—and so your statement in defense of relativity is not binding.

- You can't know anything.
  Do you know that?

- No one can know anything about God.
  Do you know that about God? To assert that God is unknowable is to say a lot about God.

- Everyone's opinion is equally valid.
  Well, my opinion is that your opinion is wrong, so your view is false; thus, not everyone's opinion is equally valid.

- What's true for you is not true for me.
  Well, what's true for me is that you are wrong.

- I feel that I'm right.
  I feel that I'm right, and I say you are wrong.

- Logic is just sophistry and isn't always true.
  You're using logic to attempt to disprove logic.

- There are no laws of logic.
  The attempt to refute the laws of logic requires the employment of the laws of logic. Logic is an invariant and universal truth. The laws of logic are nomaterial, invariant, transcendent, universal, and necessary; they require God because He is nonmaterial, immutable, transcendant, and necessary.

- The only true knowledge of reality is discovered through the positive sciences.
  That statement is not true because it is not found in the positive sciences.

- We can't be married to any idea.
  Are you married to that idea?

- Philosophy can add nothing to science.
  Is that your philosophy for your science?

- Philosophy about science is not a meaningful enterprise.
  Does that philosophical assertion of science have any meaning?

- How to Believe in Nothing and Set Yourself Free (title of a book).
  Is that what you believe?

- Language is not useful for a definition.
  Is that your definition in which you employ language?

- I can't believe in anything that I can't see or feel.
  Can you see or feel the point of that statement?

- All knowledge begins with experience.
  Did you experience that?

- God is indescribable.
  Is that your description of God?

- All speculations of the reality of absolutes are an illusion.
  Is that statement an absolute? If it is, it is an illusion, thus it is false.

- Everything is just an illusion.
  Then that statement is an illusion, so it is false. Thus all things are not illusions. If the people who hold this Eastern worldview really believed this, they wouldn't look both ways when crossing

the street. But they do, proving they can't consistently hold this view. They must depend on the Christian worldview.

- "Pundits all make over $50,000, so they can't understand anything" (Chris Matthews, wealthy pundit).
  Chris, do you understand that?

- "All knowledge is confined to the realm of experience." (Kant)
  Have you experienced all knowledge?

- The whole notion of truth must be scrapped and replaced by the ongoing process of refutation.
  Then that statement is not true.

- Every assertion is false.
  Then that assertion is false.

- I believe only in science and the scientific method.
  Is that statement scientifically testable?

- No truth is immutable.
  Then that statement is mutable, so it is not true.

- True knowledge is the only knowledge which we experience.
  Did you experience that statement?

- Truth can never be rationally attained but remains an elusive myth and an erroneous pre-commitment.
  Then that is an elusive myth and is not true.

- True knowledge is only that knowledge that can be empirically verified.
  Can you empirically verify that statement?

- Reality is not fixed, hard, and foundational.
  Is that statement fixed, hard, and foundational?

- "That intelligence, when frozen in dogmatic social

philosophy generates a vicious cycle of blind oscillation"
(Dewey).
*Is that statement frozen in dogmatic philosophy? If yes, it's blind
oscillation, and therefore is false.*

- Truth is not a boxy, dogmatic thing with hard corners
attached by dogmatists.
Are you dogmatic about that?

- Truth does not consist of words, propositions, or
assertions that can be communicated by language.
Are those words or assertions communicated by language?

- Truth depends upon your experience.
*Did you experience that proposition? No. Then it is false on its
own terms.*

- Here we have no rules.
Is that your rule?

- Lies, lies, everywhere you turn are lies.
Is that a lie?

- We and our existences are non-existences.
Does that statement exist?

- We can only discover truth by testing and
experimentation.
Are you able to test that assertion?

- Apart from mathematics, we can know nothing for sure.
*Is that proposition a mathematical equation? No. Then you are
providing in what you say the very basis to reject what you
say.*

- I enjoy the sound of silence.
Silence is the absence of sound.

- Commit to the flames any propositions or assertions
that do not contain mathematics or facts obtained from
observable experiments.

Did you test that statement with experiments or does that statement contain mathematics? No. Then commit it to the flames on its own basis.

- The only genuine knowledge is obtained by the positive sciences.
  Is that proposition verified by the positive sciences? No. Then it self-destructs and saws off the limb it was sitting on.

- We can know nothing about reality.
  Do you know that about reality?

- Sin is the outcome of knowledge.
  Do you know that? If you do, then it's sin. Sin is missing the mark or an error, therefore your statement is false.

- "The line of demarcation between knowledge and mere opinion is determined by one criterion: falsebility by empirical evidence, by observed phenomena" (Karl Popper).
  Did you observe that? If not, then that is just mere opinion.

- Knowledge is what our peers let us get away with saying.
  Your peers have decided they will not let you get away with that statement, so it's false.

- "Our religious association is free from all mixture of human opinions and inventions of men" (Alexander Campbell, in describing the anti-creed position of the Church of Christ movement).
  Is that your human opinion?

- The only thing that is predictable is unpredictability.
  Do you think that prediction is unpredictable?

- Only things that are blue are true.
  Is that statement blue?

- I doubt everything.
  If you tried to doubt everything, you would be clipping off the

rope you're holding onto, because the notion of doubting itself presupposes certainty.

- Nothing can be ultimately justified.
  Is that statement ultimately justified?

- There are no good reasons for holding to the belief in objective knowledge.
  Is that objective knowledge?

- We cannot achieve certainty because it is based on postulates.
  Are you certain about that postulate?

- Nobody's right.
  Are you right?

- Every attempt to fashion an absolute philosophy of truth and right is a delusion.
  Is that true and right?

- All I believe in are the laws of logic.
  Is that statement one of the laws of logic?

- Everyone's opinion is equally valid.
  Is that assertion more equal than others? My opinion is that assertion is false.

- All knowledge comes from observation.
  Have you observed all knowledge? The assertion does not make possible its own ground of proof.

- The whole world is an illusion.
  If that assertion were true, then it is also an illusion, so it is false. The whole world is not an illusion.

- Nothing is good or evil.
  Then that statement is not good, thus it is false.

- All English sentences consist of four words.

*This sentence comments on all English sentences, including itself;
it fails to meet its own demands, thus it is false.*

- Seen on display in a store: "I Love You Only" Valentine
  cards:
  Now available in multipacks.

- My philosophy is that if it isn't difficult, it isn't worth
  doing.
  *That is easy to say, so according to your philosophy you should
  not have uttered it. If you must utter it, speak it while you are
  crawling backwards up a mountain blindfolded.*

Turning the self-refuting statement on itself demonstrates that
it is absurd. Suppose you walked into a public restroom and on the
wall of the stall someone had written: "The proposition written on
the other side is false." You step out and read what is written on that
side and it says: "The proposition on the other side of the wall is true."
The self-refuting assertion, on its own grounds, demonstrates that
it is false and is reduced to absurdity. If it is true, it is false. It is like
trying to ride two horses going in the opposite direction at the same
time. The views within the statement have assertions that lead to
their own destruction. Christianity is the only system of thought that
is self-consistent. All non-Christian systems are self-contradictory,
inconsistent, incoherent, and self-nullifying; beyond that, Christianity
is the precondition for the intelligibility of our world and all that is in it.
The attempt to refute Christianity actually concedes the inevitability
of the Christian faith because Christianity has to be true to attempt
its denial. The employment of logic and morality in striving to refute
Christianity is an implicit acknowledgment of the absolute certainty of
God. The Christian has absolute intellectual certainty. Any comment,
premise, theory, or assertion that contradicts a universal truth in the
Bible is self-refuting and self-impaling.

Therefore let all the house of Israel know for certain that
God has made this Jesus, whom you crucified, both Lord and
Christ (Acts 2:36).

Those who have had the opportunity to witness to numerous
people know that one of the main tenets of modernity is relativism, the
self-refuting philosophy that asserts "all things are relative." Spin-offs

of this philosophy include: "What is true for you isn't true for me" and "You can't know anything for sure." These statements cannot be true because, if they were, they would invalidate themselves. If they were true, they would be false. The late University of Chicago philosophy professor Allan Bloom, in his insightful book *The Closing of the American Mind,* bemoans the fact that "there is one thing a professor can be absolutely certain of: almost every student entering the university believes, or says he believes, that truth is relative."[7] I have to agree with Bloom. I have found (having spent much time exchanging ideas on university campuses in America) that the only thinking tool most students have developed is the art of avoiding the tough questions. Out of one side of their mouth, students declare that all things are relative, then defend the truth of environmentalism out of the other. They know that relativism is not true! Obviously, relativism is a self-voiding notion, but students just do not want to be tough-minded and think through life's important issues.

Opinions Are Just That

> Pronounce them guilty, O God; let them fall by their own counsels; cast them out in the multitude of their transgressions; for they have rebelled against You (Psalms 5:10).

If you throw around the slogan "All things are relative," I want to ask you whether mistreating slaves is wrong, or murdering homosexuals is wrong, or dumping nuclear waste in the ocean is wrong? Almost every relativist will agree that those things are wrong. Christians can objectively decry the mistreatment of humans and the environment, because we know that God told us not to abuse people and nature. But those who deny absolute truth and values cannot decry them and still live consistently within the boundaries of that philosophy. No one can consistently live out a life based on relativism. They will inevitably stand for something: human rights, the right to vote, or something that is of great value to them. Once they assert that something should or should not be done, they have borrowed from the Christian worldview. No other worldview can give an unchanging, perpetual, universal, and absolute standard for ethics and morality. All systems of ethics and science will ultimately be relative except for Christianity. The Christian ethical law is based on the eternal, unchanging, and absolute nature of God. All other systems are based on opinion — the opinion of the masses or men of letters. Either way, it is their opinion, and opinions change. There are some absolutes, some things that are immutably true, some things that are not subject to opinion.

Absolutes are established on God's nature and His law. If someone tries to assert that there are no absolutes, he must use an absolute statement. This, as we have now learned, is self-impaling. If it is true, it is false. The only absolutes that are not self-refuting are those from God. So anytime relativists assert that something is true universally and immutably, they are wrong if they stand on a non-Christian foundation; their own worldview cannot provide unchanging, universal, and absolute truth. The truth found in Christ devastates and demolishes all vain imaginations.

Casting down arguments, and every high thing that exalts itself against the knowledge of God, bringing every thought into captivity to the obedience of Christ (2 Corinthians 10:4-5).

Dr. Robert Morey dismisses atheism with a powerful illustration. Morey instructs the atheist to put a dot on a piece of paper, and tells the atheist that the dot represents himself. He then tells him to draw a circle around the dot. Morey goes on to explain: "Inside the circle is all you know. Everything that you have ever learned." He asks the atheist, "How much knowledge would you say you have of all things?" If the atheist claims knowledge of one percent, Morey tells him to put one percent in the circle. He explains that this is a much larger amount than the atheist really knows. "But let's say this is what you know. Now how much knowledge is outside the circle?" The atheist responds, "Ninety-nine percent." Morey then places an X outside the circle. He then puts the atheist on the spot and poses the problem: "This X represents God. Is it possible that God exists in that ninety-nine percent of the knowledge that you admit you do not have?" The atheist has to answer, "Yes" or run. He is now a professed agnostic and no longer can claim to be an atheist. The point of the illustration: It is impossible for a true atheist to exist. This exercise totally debunks the idea of atheism. Philosophically, atheism is impossible, because it is possible for God to exist in a sphere beyond our limited personal contact. Only someone who is omnipresent would know that there is no God anywhere. Only God can be omnipresent; only God could know there was no God.

Answering An Attack

Robert Ingersoll promulgated the following Bible attack list. The refutation is written under his false statement:

1.   The Bible is cruel.
     By what standard do you measure cruelty? Deny God's word and you deny the possibility of a standard that can claim that something is cruel.

2.   The Bible is impure.
     By what standard do you measure purity? Deny God's word and you deny the possibility for moral purity, including the claim that something is impure. Purity presupposes God. God and His word are the precondition for purity.

3.   The Bible is contradictory.
     This statement assumes the laws of logic. Logic presupposes God. Deny God and you deny logic.

4.   The Bible is unscientific.
     Science assumes induction. Induction presupposes God. Deny God and you must deny induction, which is the foundation for science.

God Is True

Jesus said to him, "I am the way, the truth, and the life" (John 14:6).

In the matter of just and unjust, fair and foul, good and evil, which are the subjects of our present consultation, ought we follow the opinion of many and to fear them; or the opinion of the many who has understanding? (Plato quoting Socrates).

[L]et God be true, and every man a liar (Romans 3:4).

To have a consistent and functional worldview, one must have absolute standards and laws. If one asserts laws that do not come from God's revealed word, these assertions will be self-contradictory and self-defeating. When the non-Christian claims that there are no absolutes, he is asserting an absolute standard and a law, a standard that is self-stultifying. The statement that there are no absolutes is an absolute statement. This statement is a contradiction and self-refuting; for it to be true, it would have to be false, therefore it can only be false. There must be absolutes in logic and in morality, or we can assert nothing and account for nothing; such a thing would be impossible.

Unchanging standards do not reside in matter and cannot be empirically quantified, examined, or put into a flask. They cannot be human conventions or subjective theories made up by mutable man. The absolutes of ethics transcend time, space, and matter and cannot be tested in a lab. But all labs assume absolutes and use them in all their science. They cannot solely be the result of neuron firings in the brain, because that would make them mutable, and by definition they would not be laws. The materialist cannot explain where laws come from or justify them. If one claims there are no absolutes, one is employing absolutes to make the claim. Again, that means the claim is self-negating.

A Discussion on Truth

It has been said that "Reality is that which doesn't go away when you stop thinking about it." There is a real reality. The contrary is impossible. When a person claims that there is no reality, he is a real person talking to another real person, and that situation presupposes reality. Yet many deceived people attempt to deny the undeniable. The following is a conversation I had with a young man who professed not to believe in absolute truth:

Mike:	Hello, here is a tract that will tell you about God.
Jim:	Well, I have my own religion. I believe that everyone has their own truth, and you shouldn't push your religion on others.
Mike:	How do you know that is true?
Jim:	I believe it is true.
Mike:	How do you know that?
Jim:	I just know. It's for me. There is no truth out there, anyway.

Mike: Is that true?

Jim: Well, I told you that I do not want you pushing your religion down my throat.

Mike: As of this moment, I haven't told you anything about Jesus Christ. I haven't told you that you have broken God's law by not keeping the Ten Commandments and that you and I, without Jesus, are doomed to hell for lying, stealing, cheating, avoiding Church, using ungodly anger, coveting, and many other sins. I did not exhort you to repent and trust in Christ. I did not recount the glories of His death and resurrection. Now I have, but I haven't "pushed" it down your throat.

Jim: I do not believe a word of what you said. I told you, there is nothing that is true.

Mike: Again, I ask you, is that true?

Jim: Ah—

Mike: And how do you know that there is no truth?

Jim: I just do.

Mike: In your worldview, one could not forbid the torture of minorities and the plundering of third-world countries by the superpowers. If there is no truth, you cannot declare that anything is right or wrong. And you will have to give up science, medicine, school, governments, and everything else that is assumed to be "true."

Jim: No, I believe that the West is wrong when it subjugates third-world countries and rapes their natural resources.

Mike: Why is that wrong? By what standard do you assert that anything is wrong?

Jim: Well, it just is.

Mike: It just is? You cannot account for your claim. You must live strictly on blind irrational faith. Let me ask you another question: Where   does mathematics come from?

Jim: I don't know.

Mike: Where do the laws of logic come from?

Jim: I don't know.

Mike: Where does your personality come from?

Jim: I don't know and I do not care!

Mike: It is very apparent that you do not have any answers. You should humble yourself and learn from God's word.

Jim: I do not believe in that.

Mike: That's strange, because the Bible can supply all the answers to the questions you cannot answer. Yet you want to avoid the Bible.

Jim: I have my opinion and you have yours.

Mike: Not really. My opinion is based on God's word. His word is the precondition for logic, science, mathematics, morality, and personhood. God's pure word alone provides the necessary preconditions for all the questions and answers in life. You, in contrast, have no answers for anything. It is not a matter of opinions; it is a matter of truth. You do not have the truth. God's word is the truth.

Jim: Well, I'll just do my best.

Mike: You need to turn from your ways, flee to Jesus and away from hell. Christ will save your soul and transform your life. Christianity will also supply the only worldview that can give you a foundation for declaring evil actions as evil and truth as true. Without Christ, you have proven you cannot make sense out of this world. You are living in an inconsistent and messed-up worldview, and you need to come to Christ.

Jim: No thank you.

Mike: You are now left in a life philosophy that can supply no answers, no truth, and no morals. I have demonstrated that your view of life is self-refuting and absurd, and it will lead you to hell. Is this what you want?

Jim: I'm happy where I am.

Mike: Well, read that tract when you have a chance. I will pray for you.

Is There A Right and Wrong?

Many of the unredeemed are relativists who believe that no one is right or wrong and that morality is based on individual taste. This belief is a huge problem in America and the Western world. The following is a fictitious conversation compiled by combining many real conversations I have had with others.

Christian: The Bible instructs humanity that homosexual acts are evil.

Relativist: I believe that there is no right or wrong. And you should not push your morals on me.

Christian: Do you think I'm wrong in doing that?

Relativist: Yes!

Christian: Well, you just insisted that there is no right or wrong, yet you scolded me, and told me I was wrong in my moral view about homosexuality.

Relativist: I just think that you shouldn't force your morality on me.

Christian: Are you forcing that moral view on me?

Relativist: O.K. You shouldn't push your moral views on others.

Christian: Why not?

Relativist: Because it is wrong.

Christian: Again, I remind you that you said that there is no right or wrong.

Relativist: I only insist that you do not push your morality on others.

Christian: Are you still pushing that morality on me? And are you saying that we should let large industrial corporations burn down the rain forests?

Relativist: No way; that would be evil!

Christian: Would you want to push that morality on those big corporations that want to burn down the rain forests and damage the environment? If you claim that there is no right or wrong, you are also saying that the abuse of women, the murder of children, and the enslavement of minorities aren't wrong. But you need to know that discussing morals is not a game. If we reject God's word, we are left with sinful men making personal moral decisions based on selfish gain. There must be moral absolutes to distinguish virtue from vice, right from wrong, and good from evil. If there is no objective moral standard, all manner of evil will flourish.

God Is An Exact God

The Triune God of glory is an exact God. Precision, truth, and judgment presuppose an exact God. Only the God of the Bible is exact and true. God's geometry is exact: There is a square square, a triangular triangle, a circular circle. Geometry presupposes a transcendent God because nowhere in our physical universe can one find a perfect square, triangle, or circle. They exist in the perfect state in theory and they exist only in theory in this world. Yet mathematics has proven that there are perfect squares, circles, and triangles. Why do we have an abstract principle that does not exist in the physical world? An atheist cannot give an answer to this problem. Ask the skeptic: "Why are there not perfect geometric entities in our world, when they exist in theory?" The only objective basis one can find for perfect circles, squares, and triangles is a perfect God who transcends our imperfect world. Mathematical theorems assert that there are infinite numbers. Yet there is nothing infinite in our physical world. Infinite numbers do not exist in our physical reality. Only an infinite God can justify the truth of infinite numbers.

God is also the precondition for time. Everyone knows that time exists in the past, present, and future. We believe that time passes. This belief may appear to be self-evident, but time can only be justified by presupposing God. It is 11:55:57 seconds before the second hand reaches 58 seconds. The second can go infinitely forward and can seemingly never end. 57.1 seconds, then 57.2, 57.3, and on and on forever. I can break that time down by asking: Did it ever become 11:55 and 57.1 seconds? 57.12 seconds? Yes. 57.123, and on and on in an infinite progression. Hence without the Trinity as the source and foundation for the one and many, I cannot even account for time. Without the infinite God, who is the foundation for infinite numbers, the non-Christian cannot solve this paradox. This is not a problem for the Trinitarian, because he believes in an infinite and eternal God. Non-Christians use infinite numbers, yet these numbers have no end; hence, they do not comport with their worldview. One must presuppose the Triune God. The unbeliever cannot even account for time. Each second, God is an exact God, and time presupposes this God.

The Mire of Mere Assertion

People can declare anything they want, but the mere declaration does not make a declaration true. Suppose you borrowed ten thousand dollars from a relativist and when it was time to pay it back, you told him that the ten thousand dollars was just twenty dollars to you. All things are relative! Ten thousand dollars may be true to you, but it is not true for me; twenty dollars is. This approach will bring out the inconsistencies of the relativist, as well as a red and livid face. As the steam is blowing out of his ears, ask him whether you can drop a fifty-pound rock on his foot, because the rock, to you, is light as a feather. He will not go for that any more than he will allow you to not pay him all the money you owe him. He may state that all things are relative and that what is true for him is not true for you, but he cannot live out his worldview. The Christian can. We know that God has commanded us not to steal and that He has made our world, so that what is ultimately true is true for everyone. One plus one is always two, no matter who or where you are. Mathematics and all absolutes are justified from God. People can assert anything; however, the assertion itself does not make it true. The assertion must be justified and valid to be true. Without the Bible one cannot justify anything. God's word alone supplies truth and the means to discern truth.

Transcribed below is a conversation I had with a gentleman who was stuck in the "mire of mere assertion":

Mike:	How's it going? Do you have a moment to talk about God?
George:	The cosmos is God
Mike:	How do you know that? That statement is arbitrary.
George:	Well, the Christian God is false.
Mike:	How do you know that?
George:	The Bible has been corrupted through the ages.
Mike:	How do you know that?
George:	We know UFO's have come and the backward

	people of the Bible thought that the aliens were God.

Mike: How do you know that? That statement is arbitrary.

George: Well, the pyramids tell us that aliens came and seeded the earth.

Mike: Again, how do you know that?

George: I hate getting into religious quarrels. All religions are basically the same anyway.

Mike: How do you know that? That statement is also arbitrary.

George: You keep saying that!

Mike: Yes. Anytime a person asserts something that is not based on the truth of the Bible, that assertion is unjustifiable. They will be stuck in the mire of mere assertion. One's assertion doesn't make anything true. If anyone says something contrary to scripture, all I have to ask them is: "How do you know that?" They will have no way to account for their opinions, when those opinions conflict with God's word. And your assertions are just the opinion of a man, and they are arbitrary and can't be rationally justified.

George: Well, that's just your opinion.

Mike: No, my worldview is based on the Holy Bible. The Bible provides justification for my beliefs. It is impossible for the Bible not to be true. Without God's word you cannot account for logic, reason, morality, induction, and mathematics. God is the precondition for the intelligibility of this world. All assertions must be based on God's word and the principles that come from it.

George: The Bible is not the only truth.

Mike: How do you know that?

George: I'll see you later.

Mike: Think about what I said. Without God you cannot account for anything in this world. Jesus is the truth. I'll pray that some day you will turn and trust in Him.

I have had many conversations like the one above. This kind of confrontation is a good way to demonstrate to the unbeliever that his opinion is meaningless and absurd, if it conflicts with scripture. Ask the unbeliever: "How do you know that?" This question will demonstrate that he has no justifiable answers and that his claims are arbitrary.

Autonomous Reason

Mankind has demonstrated throughout history its propensity to attempt to rely on autonomous reason. We desire to rule ourselves, without God's revelation, by depending on reason alone. Yes, we should think and behave "rationally." We are logically obligated to be rational. But as soon as you attempt to deny reason, you must use reason to assert that denial. A man cannot deny his rational nature without refuting himself. He must resort to employing reason, even in the vain attempt to resist rationality. No matter how much philosophical ingenuity he employs in denying reason, he must always use reason to do so. And the only foundation for reason is God and His revelation. Deny God, and one has no immutable source of reason and logic. This is no empty claim; without God there is no reason to trust our reason. We can trust human reason only when it is built on the foundation of God and His revelation.

An Alien Experiment?

The trouble with the worldview of the nonbeliever is that it cannot account for any idea or object in the universe. The nonbeliever cannot prove that he is not just a super hi-tech computer chip in an alien Pentium computer—an entity that does not really exist but only thinks he does, a matrix machine that believes it is a human. If you ask an unbeliever, "How do you know that you are not an alien computer chip?" he cannot give you proof, unless he presupposes the truth of scripture. The Bible reveals who we are and what God's plan is for mankind, and it is impossible for the Bible not to be true. All my questions and speculations, and even science fiction, presuppose that God lives and has revealed himself to men.

Many atheists attempt to label religious faith as a crutch. They charge that theists are afraid of death and that God is just a projection of our own need to comfort that fear. Again, for any statement regarding anything to be rational, God must live. God is the precondition for any investigation or rational discourse. The claim that Jesus is a crutch in one sense is true, but I would go even further. Jesus is not just my crutch, He is my wheelchair. Without His grace and strength I could not live a full and healthy life. When a nonbeliever pushes the pyschobabble assertion that the only reason we believe is because of fear or psychological weakness, we can turn this argument around. That type of statement is a double-edged sword. I tell the unbeliever that they reject God because of fear. They know that hell exists and they are afraid of its reality, so they convince themselves that God does not exist; they do this for the comfort of their minds. God's nonexistence is a projection of their minds because of fear, so they actively suppress the truth of God in their mind. Darwin said that Christianity was a "damnable doctrine" because he despised the thought of hell.

> Serpents, brood of vipers, how can you escape the condemnation of hell? (Matthew 23:33).

The foundation for absolutes is found only in scripture. The Bible is true. Christianity alone can account for logic and reason. No other worldview can supply the preconditions needed for discerning truth. The Bible must be true, if anything is true. Numerous self-deceivers, infidels, profligates, and wreckers have assaulted the Bible. Thomas Paine exerted much intellectual labor against scripture (as though he would receive high commissions in reward for his critiques). Yet when he was confronted and asked whether he owned a Bible, he admitted that he did not have one in his house or study. Many have tried to destroy the Holy Bible: Hume, Voltaire, and Bertrand Russell have all tried their hand at it. All their critical essays and books are in reality faith-builders for the Christian. Their writings fortify our faith in that all their criticisms presuppose God and scripture. Thus their attacks against the Bible need the Bible to furnish an ultimate foundation that allows them to issue their arguments. The God of Holy Writ is the necessary precondition for intelligible argument. He is the precondition of all criticism and intellectual attack. Calvin said of scripture, "The beauties of scholars and philosophers will almost entirely disappear; so that it is easy to perceive something divine in sacred scripture, which far surpasses the highest attainments and ornaments of human industry." That is true, but the truth goes beyond that. All philosophy, even errant philosophy, presupposes God and His revelation. Without God, one cannot justify the use of reason, logic, and ethics that the godly and ungodly philosophers marshal in their postulations and theories.

One needs God to attempt to refute God. The nineteenth-century British author and Christian apologist G. K. Chesterton said, "To disbelieve in God would be like waking up in the morning, looking in the mirror and seeing nothing." To see and to understand anything, one must stand on the Christian worldview. God must be, or we cannot make sense of any fundamental phenomenon. No wonder the infidel philosopher John Stuart Mill acknowledged on his deathbed that atheism never gave him any "peace, comfort, of consolation." He admitted that his life in opposition to Christianity was a failure. An unbeliever, when asked to account for logic or morality, can only say: "They just are" or "They are solely the result of molecules and motion; the physical world alone gave us these nonphysical dynamics." These statements cannot be true, because if true they would not be so universally or unalterably; logic and morality would have no transcendent foundation, and would undermine everything logic and morality assert. All propositions would be unintelligible, self-refuting, and untrue. Christianity is true, and any attempt to refute it will always lead to rational self-destruction. The non-Christian cannot contend against God in view of the fact that he has fighting instruments that come only from the Christian arsenal. He must unsheathe God's logic, morality, and induction to battle God. He needs God to propose anything that opposes God. Deny God and all is unintelligible. It is impossible for the Christian faith not to be true.

God Must Exist

It is impossible for God not to exist. He is the precondition for the intelligibility of all reality. It is not just that our DNA code presupposes thought, and thought a thinker. It is not just that the universe appears to be designed, and a design presupposes a designer and a plan a planner. I believe and affirm all this, but I am a Christian and everything I see in the world is proof of God's existence. The skeptic does not hold the same presuppositions as I do. Hume demonstrated the fallacy of arguing for God's existence by the use of proofs. It is brain-straining to believe, as atheists do, that something came from nothing, order from chaos, harmony from discord, and life from non-life. I do not have enough faith to believe in such nonsense. Our solar system is not an accident any more than a wristwatch is one; but this is not convincing to a skeptic who holds atheistic presuppositions. God exists, and it is impossible for Him not to exist. Even the discussion of His existence presupposes that God lives. Without God, one cannot account for the logic used in any conversation regarding the existence of God.

The Bible does not just give us a rational reason to be confident in God's existence. God is not a probability; He is alive and He is the precondition for all rational thought. He is not a mere probability. He must live, or everything is meaningless and absurd—which would mean that statement itself is absurd and therefore fallacious. God lives, and He does not need any proof. Everything is proof. There is no doubt in that God is there and He is not silent. Even if I fall into doubt, my doubt uses logic, so even my doubt presupposes God. It is like the story of the little girl who was being ridiculed for believing in the Bible and the story of Jonah. She said to the scoffer, "I believe every word in the Bible. I know Jonah survived in the belly of a whale, and I'll ask him how he survived when I get to heaven and see him there." The skeptic then asked her, "What if Jonah isn't there?" She replied, "Then you ask him." Simple faith is not just simple, it is also powerful. God gives us faith, and without Him and His word nothing in the world would be intelligible.

God's Law Identifies Evil

God has been conceived as the foundation of the metaphysical situation with its ultimate activity. If this conception be adhered to, there can be no alternative except to discern in Him the origin of evil as well as good.[8]

The syllogism which states

1.   If God were all-good and all powerful, He would defeat evil;
2.   Evil exists;
3.   Therefore God does not exist

Is fallacious because the syllogism itself presupposes God. The argument itself depends on God's existence. Even an argument against God's existence depends upon the Lord to propose it. The argument from evil that attempts to disprove God's existence utilizes logic, morality, and a distinction between good and evil. God is the precondition for logic and morality. He is the basis for making a distinction between good and evil. Without God, everything just is. There can be no objective moral truths, or truths of any kind. When a man asserts good and evil, he presupposes that God lives.

Most atheists frame the argument of evil like this:

1. If God is all-good and all-powerful, He would defeat evil.
2. Evil is not defeated.
3. Therefore, God does not exist.

The transcendental argument demonstrates that this argument presupposes God. But the syllogism itself is not even valid. A Christian should never accept the syllogism as written above. The way we should pose the formula is:

1. If God is all-good and all-powerful, He can defeat evil.
2. Evil is not yet defeated.
3. Therefore, God will defeat evil in the future.

The Bible testifies that one day God will rid the world of evil. Evil will be defeated. When one makes an argument, one has God as the ultimate ground for the logic employed in the argument, including an argument from evil. The Christian is to examine the argument and only accept it if it is consistent with the teaching of scripture. The atheist has no way of knowing that God will not defeat evil sometime in the future. The believer has God's word on it. The atheist is left holding an empty bag, a bag that God made. The grounds from which an atheist attacks God are based on God's revelation. The atheist must borrow from the Christian worldview to attempt to disprove God. Only in the context of the Christian worldview are good and evil intelligible. The existence of God is well beyond just a reasonable proof. God is the foundation for knowing anything at all. Deny God and one cannot make sense out of anything, including good and evil.

Give Answers with Meekness and Respect

One must never respond to questions about evil in a nonchalant, callous, or detached way. One must have compassion for those who struggle with this paradox. Many of those who focus on this question have lost loved ones through criminal actions, disease, or natural disasters. A post-September 11th Barna survey found:

Those who believe in an all-powerful, all-knowing God dropped from 72% pre-attack to 68% afterward.
Confidence in absolute moral truths dropped from 38% to 22%.

Truth can transform, and it is beautiful. Love rejoices in the truth, but truth is more than that. Truth is fully true and is not false. Some things are objectively true, regardless of whether we like them or not. One should stand for the truth, but with the understanding that truth is not just a matter of academic debate. There are real, hard-hitting, and unpleasant issues one must tackle with love and humility.

Certainty is Certain

If the Christian worldview is not true, then knowledge is impossible. The only way to avert skepticism is to have an unchanging, infinite, infallible, and exhaustive authority. The God of the Bible alone has these attributes. The statement that "knowledge is impossible" is a claim of knowledge, and hence is false. God is the precondition for intellectual certainty. And there must be certainty. The statement that asserts that there is no certainty is self-refuting, because it claims certainty. Hence there must be a certain, immutable, and infallible authority. That authority is God Almighty. All other starting points are self-contradictory.

Only Christianity supplies the foundation necessary for logic, science, moral standards, and mathematics. No non-Christian system of thought can furnish a foundation for the law of non-contradiction. Thus those systems of thought can only offer a self-nullifying worldview. The true God is the primordial requirement for all knowledge, proof, evidence, and logic. It is impossible for God not to exist. He is the precondition for the intelligibility of reality. He is the universal and necessary rationale. The nonphysical, transcendent, and immutable

God supplies the necessary preconditions for the use of nonphysical, transcendent, universal, and immutable logic. To argue at all, one must presuppose that God lives. Non-believing thought cannot supply the necessary preconditions for the laws of logic; hence, it results in futility because of the internal contradictions it supplies. Therefore, the contrary of Christianity is impossible. All other worldviews fall into absurdity inasmuch as they are self-contradictory and lead to conclusions that contradict their own primary assumptions. Without God, nothing can make sense. The true and living God is the pre-essential for knowledge and for the understanding of all human experience. Christianity is the inescapable truth inasmuch as it alone provides the preconditions for the universal and unchanging laws of logic. Universal and certain claims are unavoidable, and Christianity alone provides the preconditions for universal and certain claims; thus, Christianity must be true.

Notes

[1] Danny Lehmann, *Bringing Them Back Alive* (Springdale, PA.: Whitaker House, 1987), p. 46.

[2] Madeleine L'Engle, *The Genesis Trilogy* (Colorado Springs: Waterbrook Press, 1997), p. 108.

[3] Swami Prabhupada, *Krishna* (New York: Bhaktivedanta, 1970), p. 123.

[4] R. C. Sproul, John Gerstner, & Arthur Lindsey, *Classical Apologetics* (Grand Rapids: Zondervan 1984), p. 72.

[5] George Orwell, *1984* (New York: Signet, 1949), p. 228.

[6] John Frame, *The Doctrine of the Knowledge of God* (Phillipsburg, NJ: P & R, 1987), p. 63.

[7] Allan Bloom, *The Closing of the American Mind* (New York: Simon & Schuster, 1987), p. 25.

[8] Alfred North Whitehead, *Science and the Modern World* (New York: Free Press, 1925), p. 179.

CHAPTER SEVEN

THE TRINITY:
THE PROBLEM OF THE ONE AND THE
MANY SOLVED

Science has gone a very long way towards proving the essential unity of all phenomena.[1]

The Absolute may explain everything; it cannot explain anything in particular.[2]

We really believe that the deity is tri-personal — not mono-personal, but tri-personal. The doctrine teaches that there are three persons in the one Godhead, and not one.[3]

If it is necessary in our thinking about God to move to a position beyond naturalism and supra-naturalism; this is no less important in our thinking about Christ. Otherwise, we shall be shut up...to a sterile choice between the two.[4]

Tertullian gives us this definition of the Trinity: "Thus, the connection of the Father in the Son, and the Son in the Paraclete, produces three coherent Persons, who are yet distinct One from Another. These Three are one essence, not one Person, as it is said, 'I and my Father are One,' in respect to unity of substance, not singularity of number." And the Nicene Creed formulates the doctrine in this way: "We believe in one God, the Father Almighty, maker of all things...And in one Lord Jesus Christ, the Son of God, begotten of the Father; that is, of the essence of the Father, God of God, Light of Light, very God of very God...being of one substance with the Father...And in the Holy Spirit." This is the God of the Bible — the Christian Deity. From the first to the last book, the Bible declares that God is a plurality within a unity, one God in three persons. And the one true Triune God is the answer to the most paradoxical problem in the history of philosophy: How does the one and the many, unity and diversity, the plurality and the oneness relate? The Trinity alone provides the solution.

> The Trinity also means that God's creation can be both one and many. Secular philosophy veers between the two extremes of monism (the world is really one and plurality is an illusion) and pluralism (the world is radically disunited and unity is an illusion). Secular philosophy moves from one extreme to the other, because it does not have the resources to define a position between the two extremes, and because it seeks an absolute extreme or another—as if there must be an absolute oneness (with no plurality) or else a universe of unique, unconnected elements, creating an absolute pluralism and destroying universal oneness....But the Christian knows there is no absolute unity (devoid of plurality) or absolute plurality (devoid of unity)....The Christian knows that God is the only absolute, and that the absolute is both one and many. Thus, we are freed from the task of trying to find utter unity or utter disunity....When we search for ultimate criteria or standards, we look...to the living God.[5]

The Biblical Support

Following is a list of scriptures that reveal to man that God is three persons in one God. This revelation is important, since there are many cults and false religions that appeal to the Bible in their attempt to deny the Trinity. These scriptures are some of the key passages on the doctrine of the Trinity. This scripture list is incomplete, and it is recommended that you read some apologetic books on the Trinity and some books on the cults. Ron Rhodes has written a couple of fine books on the cults that discuss the Trinity at length. Dr. Robert Morey's book on the Trinity is the best on this important doctrine.

Some tri-unity scripture verses are:
Genesis 1:26, 3:22, 11:6;
Psalms 45:6-7;
Isaiah 6:8, 48:11-17;

Hosea 1:7;
Zechariah 10:12, 12:10;
Matthew 28:19;
2 Corinthians 13:14

Bible verses that reveal that God is one:
Deuteronomy 6:4;
Isaiah 43:10, 44:6, 45:5-6, 48:3-16

Scriptures that reveal that the Father is God:
Matthew 6:8;
John 4:23, 17:3;
1 John 2:23

Verses of holy writ that teach that Jesus is God:
John 1:1, 8:58, 10:30, 20:28;
Hebrews 1;
Isaiah 9:6, 7:14;
Colossians 1:15;
Acts 20:28

Bible verses that instruct us that the Holy Spirit is God:
Acts 10:19-20, 13:2, 21:11;
1 Corinthians 12:11;
Gal. 4:6;
John 15:26, 16:7;
Micah 2:7;
Isaiah 61:1, 63:10-11;
Psalms 55:11, 139:7

And without controversy great is the mystery of godliness:
God was manifest in the flesh, justified in the Spirit, seen of
angels, preached unto the Gentiles, believed on in the world,
received up into glory (1 Timothy 3:16).

Behold, he comes with clouds; and every eye shall see him, and
they also which pierced him: and all kindreds of the earth shall
wail because of him. Even so, Amen. I am Alpha and Omega,
the beginning and the ending, says the Lord, who is, and who
was, and who is to come, the Almighty (Revelation 1:7-8).

Most of the cults teach that Jesus is *heter-ousia*, a different substance or essence from the Father. But the Bible declares that Jesus is one with the Father (John 10:30). The Trinity is reasonable. However, I do not fully understand God's nature due to the fact that there will always remain some mystery about the being of God. Mysteries are not contradictions. The one true God is the Father, Son, and Holy Spirit.

The Attacks on the Trinity

Many non-Christian religions and philosophies attack the Trinity as a contradiction. They declare that the doctrine of the Trinity breaks the law of non-contradiction. David Hume, Bertrand Russell, Immanuel Kant, Muhammad, and Thomas Jefferson were critical of the Christian God. Kant declared that the Trinity "provides nothing...even if one claims to understand it." Jefferson scoffed, "When we have done away with the incomprehensible jargon of the Trinitarian arithmetic...we shall then be...worthy disciples." The reason for his mocking, irritated tone is that the unbeliever's mind is darkened and he applies the wrong arithmetic. Everyone knows that one plus one plus one equals three, not one. But what does one multiplied by one and multiplied by one equal? One. The Trinity is a mystery, but not "a mystery wrapped in a riddle inside an enigma," in the famous words attributed to Winston Churchill. God is three persons in one being. God in His almightiness is a mystery. We do not know how the doctrine of the tri-unity of God works. We just know that the Trinity is true and without the Trinity, as the one true God, we cannot make sense out of anything. Reject the Trinity and one cannot account for personhood, love, equality, mathematics, justice, morality, and logic. The Trinitarian nature of God is the precondition for understanding reality and truth. Many Christians recoil at defending the Trinity because they think it is a contradiction and a problem; rather, it is the solution. The Father is God, the Son is God, and the Holy Spirit is God. And there is only one God, three persons in one being. This concept does not break any of the laws of logic. If the doctrine taught that there are three persons in one person or three beings in one being, that would be a contradiction. The Bible teaches instead that there are three persons in one being. This doctrine is a mystery, not a contradiction. The Trinity violates no known law of logic. And remember, the mathematics of the Triune God is not $1 + 1 + 1 = 1$ but $1 \times 1 \times 1 = 1$.

We worship one God in Trinity, and Trinity in Unity; neither confounding the Persons: nor dividing the Substance. For there is one Person of the Father: another of the Son: and another of the Holy Spirit. But, the Godhead of the Father, and the Son, and the Holy Spirit, is all one: the Glory equal, the Majesty co-eternal (Athanasian Creed).

Modern Judaism, Islam, and the Jehovah's Witnesses proclaim that God is an absolute one, a monad, a unitarian deity. The famous Rabbi Rashi, in his commentary on the third day of creation, taught that before God created the universe "He was *yachid ba'olam*: all alone." Only the Christian God, the true God, did not create out of necessity but out of liberty. He is self-existent, has aseity, and needs nothing. God does not need the creation in order to have someone to care about and love. Within God Himself He is love. God is a noun and a verb. He is a Triune being actively involved within Himself and His creation. He is stupendous, magnificent, and resplendent in His infinite Triune glory. A god who has "needs" is not perfect and infinite. Such a god could not possibly exist. It is not just reasonable to believe in the deity of Christ and the Triune nature of God; the contrary is impossible. God is Trinity. The Trinity is a mystery among us, and above us, and beyond us. He dwells within all Christians by faith, and this mystery is the key to understanding our world. The sundry religious theories about God demonstrate the ineptness of man's unaided reason. Without God's revelation in His word all man-made religions create a god who is a divine monad or the plural pantheon of gods in polytheism. Mankind needs revelation to discover the only true and living God.

God is a self-complete and self-contained unity. There is but one God. God is an absolute personality. There are three persons in the Godhead: the Father, the Son, and the Holy Spirit. Within the being of God, diversity is no more fundamental than unity. God is a tri-unity. The persons of the one God are mutually eternal and exhaustive of one another. The Holy Spirit and the Son are ontologically equal with God the Father. That is the solution to the problem of the "one and the many." We baptize in the name (singular) of the Father, the Son, and the Holy Spirit (plurality). The unity of the particulars is grounded in the being of God. There is unity and a diversity in God; there is unity and diversity in the cosmos. Unity accords with diversity because, in the nature of the Triune God, there are no particulars in unequal relationship with universals. There is nothing universal that is not equal in its particulars.

God said, "Let *us* make man in *our* image and *our likeness*." No aspect of the universe is higher than the other. The unity in the universe is equal with the diversity in the universe; they are equal because the Triune God created and sustains them. All non-Christian worldviews sacrifice the unity for the diversity or the diversity for the unity. Only God in three persons can provide the solution to the problem of "the one and the many." Thus other systems of thought are false.

The Triune God Is the Only Starting Point

There are three persons in the Godhead: the Father, the Son, and the Holy Spirit and these three are one God; the same in substance, equal in power and glory (Westminster Shorter Catechism).

The God of the Bible in Trinity is the starting point for epistemology, apologetics, and philosophy. The Triune God is reflected and revealed everywhere in the material and nonmaterial worlds. The Trinity "confronts" humanity and all creation everywhere at all times. You cannot look into a microscope or a telescope or a mathematical table and fail to be confronted by the God who alone is the Father, the Son, and the Holy Spirit. The Triune God is the foundation and the solution to the problem of the one and the many. God is the solution and not the problem. Within the being of the Triune God, unity and diversity, the one and the many, are equally ultimate and infinite.

We see God in His Triune nature revealed in the Bible from Genesis to Revelation. We must declare the truth of the Father, Son, and Holy Spirit, one God in three persons, the blessed Trinity. He is not the god of the philosophers or the pagan religions. God is the Alpha and Omega, the First and the Last. We must affirm, trust, and love the true and living God. The Triune God is the solution that makes sense out of everything in the world. This is one reason the believer is to study theology. Theology is the study of God. Many Christians confess that they dislike theology and try to avoid it. As John Muether wrote in *Modern Reformation*: "For many people theology is like underwear—you need it, so you are glad you have it on, but you sure hope it doesn't show."[6] But the foundation for all reality, and for understanding that reality, is the Triune nature of God. The explanation of all entities, phenomena, things, laws, and concrete objects begins with God. Beginning with any starting point or presupposition other than the Trinity is self-defeating.

The God revealed in scripture is the standard for truth, philosophy, and science; this is not a debatable proposition. We must begin, move, and finish with God or we cannot justify anything we do. The Trinity is the solution to all questions and the source of all true knowledge. All thought presupposes the true God. That does not mean that we must only use theological rhetoric. As Gregory of Nyssa lamented in his time, "If you ask for change, someone philosophizes...on the begotten and the unbegotten. If you ask i[f] the bath [is] ready, someone answers [that] the Son of God came from nothing." Presupposing the Trinity as the solution to all questions and the standard for truth does not mean that we must construct a theological postulate just to perform mundane tasks. Yet every simple task and every piece of routine communication presupposes the Triune God, because we use logic and morality in all those endeavors. God is the precondition for all logic and morality. If we presuppose anything other than God as our starting point, we end up with absurd and contradictory affirmations. The tri-unity of God—the Father, the Son, and the Holy Spirit—is inescapable if we want to make sense out of our world. To reject the Triune God is to end up asserting philosophical demise. Deny God and you commit logical suicide.

God's Nature Reflected in Nature

And He is before all things, and in Him all things hold together (Colossians 1:17).

There is a tri-unity in the universe composed of time, space, and matter. Each aspect is comprised of its own tri-unity. In the universe these are three distinct dynamics. All three are also divided by three. Space is comprised of height, width, and depth—a tri-unity. All is space, yet a distinct aspect of space. Matter is comprised of solid, liquid, and gas which make up a tri-unity of matter. Time is past, present, and future. Each is time and is fully time. We can see God's nature reflected in His creation. The Trinity is not a problem but the solution. The Lord is the starting point and the stopping point. The Lord is the Alpha and Omega, the Beginning and the End.

Not only is the tri-unity of God not a contradiction and not a problem, but it is the solution to the intelligibility of our world. Without the Father, the Son, and the Holy Spirit as one God, we cannot account for love, motion, communication, relationships, mathematics, or any atom in the universe. God's Triune glory is reflected in His creation. A lonely monad god cannot be the solution for the problem of the one and the many, and this false god is not reflected in the creation. As Gregory Nazianzus mused, "I cannot think of the One without immediately being surrounded by the radiance of the Three; nor can I discern the Three without once being carried back to the One."

Mathematics: The Absolute Precondition —

One God in Three Persons

Your throne is established from of old; You are from everlasting (Psalms 93:2).

Mathematics has demonstrated that infinite numbers exist in theory. Only by presupposing an infinite Triune God can one justify infinite numbers. One can count 1, 2, 3, 4, and go on infinitely. One can count backwards: $-1, -2, -3, -4$, and go on infinitely in that direction. Yet our universe is finite. God is the precondition for infinite numbers. Without an infinite God one cannot account for infinite numbers. The Triune God is the precondition for making sense out of our world. The true God has to be a tri-unity. A solitary god would be unitary and alone before he created the angels or mankind; thus, love, justice, communication, relationship, and mercy cannot be necessary attributes of this god. Only the One tri-personal God of scripture can have these traits as part of His being and nature.

Great is our Lord, and mighty in power: His understanding is infinite (Psalms 147:5).

The discipline of mathematics presupposes the Father, the Son, and the Holy Spirit: One God. He is infinite; eternal; and unchangeable in His being, wisdom, power, and holiness. In the material world, we do not see the infinite. However, mathematical theory irrefutably demonstrates that infinite numbers exist in the realm of the abstract. Draw a line a foot in length. You can divide it in two. Then you can divide those two lines in two. You can repeat this abstract division, dividing the lines in two, and you will never have to stop. Mathematically, you could divide any size line forever unto infinity. Ask the unbeliever if an infinite number of marbles could exist in the universe. If he answers in the affirmative, then follow up with this question: If someone played a game of marbles and shot one of the infinite number of marbles out of the universe, what is infinity minus one? If that is not enough to get your head spinning, ask yourself: "How many squares can fit into a five-foot square?" The answer is an infinite number of squares. These types of puzzles that employ infinities do not make sense in our finite physical universe. However, mathematics has proven that there are infinites. The materialist, who claims only the physical, material world exists, cannot account for infinite numbers in a finite world consisting only of material things. Infinite lines and entities could not exist in a world of only material things.

> How precious also are Your thoughts to me, O God! How great is the sum of them! If I should count them, they would be more in number than the sand: when I awake, I am still with You (Psalms 139:17-18).

Christ sustains and holds all things together. For this reason mathematical truth applies to the physical sciences and physics. Christ lays the foundation so that rational mankind can trust and utilize mathematics and physics. The diverse parts (the many) and the specific applications (the one) of mathematics agree with one another because of the tri-unity of God. Without God, one could not study mathematics, because it is a theological study of the unity and the diversity in our world. The eternal and infinite God is the absolute precondition that makes mathematics possible.

The use of mathematics and logic requires morality. Disclaim God and His moral law and there is no obligation to affirm that two plus two equal four and that "A" cannot be "A" and "Non-A" at the same time and in the same way. Must I affirm mathematical or logical truth? If so, I must provide objective and unchanging moral grounds for the obligation. And that requires an unchanging God. For two plus three not to be four, anywhere at any time, requires a universal truth which presupposes an all-knowing God who supplies the moral law. God's law commands all men to tell the truth and forbids lying. This is the reason we "ought" to affirm two plus three equal five.

God: A Projection? A Crutch?

Many skeptics frequently hurl the charge that God is simply a projection of one's imagination. They argue that Christians have a lack or a wanting in their lives, some type of psychological co-dependence syndrome that needs to be filled with belief in a benevolent God. God is just a crutch and Christians have psychologically projected God to fulfill their needs. The problem with this explanation is that the Biblical God is not the type of God we would make up. People create a god in their own image. The Muslims create a bloodthirsty god for a bloodthirsty culture. New Agers create a god like themselves: A sinner who lacks the attributes of righteousness, justice, and holiness. The average secular American creates a god who is a mellow combination of Santa Claus, Samantha Stephens of *Bewitched*, the Force, and Seth. The holy and awesome God, who makes men tremble, is not the type one would invent.

The God of scripture is not a God that one would make up if left to himself. Christian theology declares a revelation from a source that transcends mankind. Christians must proclaim that God is the Father, and the Son, and the Holy Spirit; one God, unique, and indivisible; alone in majesty, clothed in splendor, might, and holiness. The Triune God reveals so much of His nature that is awesome and frightening, righteous and unbending. So much of the sovereign God is mysterious and overwhelming. Even some Christians attempt to apologize for God's attributes, and many professed believers are unwilling to follow Him. They want to make Him more "seeker-friendly." They attempt to do a little tinkering with His character, so that God comes across more acceptably to them. We must resist this compromise with all that we are and proclaim from the housetops: I believe in God, the Father Almighty, Maker of the heavens and the Earth, I believe in His dear Son, and I believe in the Holy Spirit. This is our God, and He is almighty.

God Is Love

Love suffers long, and is kind; love does not envy; love does not parade itself, is not puffed up, does not behave rudely, does not seek its own, is not provoked, thinks no evil; does not rejoice in iniquity, but rejoices in the truth; bears all things, believes all things, hopes all things, endures all things. Love never fails....And now abide faith, hope, love, these three; but the greatest of these is love (1 Corinthians 13:4-13).

A tough question for the unbeliever: What is love? Is it a pat on the head, a hug, and the kiss of a loved one? If yes, one can ask the question: When your loved one is too busy to hug or kiss you, does he now not love you? All men know that real love transcends the material world. Yet many claim that love is just the chemical firing of neurons in the brain. If so, why do we love and miss our loved ones when they die? Love not only points clearly to God, but without God one cannot account for love. The Bible defines love much differently than the secular world. Love does not seek its own but rejoices in the truth and never fails. God is love. Love springs from the Triune Lord. God's inter-personal, reciprocal, and communal love is within the Godhead. We are created in the image of God; thus, we have love, give love, and seek love.

Islam Confronted by the Truth of the Trinity

A Muslim man overheard a discussion on Islam I was having with a friend. He interrupted and engaged us in the following conversation:

Muslim: If you guys are concerned about Muhammad's holy wars, you need to know that the Christians engaged in the Crusades and other horrors.

Mike: I would agree that many men who claimed to be Christians committed wicked acts in war and other atrocities. The difference between Islam and Christianity is that the founder of Islam commanded his followers to wage war, and he led many bloody wars himself, while the founder of Christianity commanded his people to be loving and just. Jesus never led a military war, and He commanded His followers to love their enemies. If a Muslim goes to war in the name of Islam and kills people because they will not convert, he is being consistent with his religion. If the Christian murders people who refuse to convert in the name of God, he is doing the exact opposite of what he is commanded to do.

Muslim: Well, you believe in three Gods.

Mike: No. We believe in the Trinity. Can you define the Trinity?

Muslim: It is three Gods that are one God. It doesn't make sense.

Mike: No. That is not the proper definition of the God of the Bible. He is three persons in one God. He is not three gods in one God or three persons in one person. The Trinity is the doctrine that declares three persons in one God; this does not break the logical law of non-contradiction.

Muslim: Tell me, what is one plus one plus one?

Mike: Well, the better question that I have for you: What is one times one times one?

Muslim: One.

Mike: Exactly. Not only is the Trinity logical, it is impossible for God not to be the Father, the Son, and the Holy Spirit, one God. Let me ask you a question: If God is just a monad, a single-person God, where did love come from? Who did Allah love before he created the angels or men? Love needs an object. Allah and all monad deities cannot have love as a basic part of their nature. Only the Triune God of scripture is true and living.

Muslim: Well, I can't answer your question right now.

Mike: Let me ask you another question. Where did the notion of equality come from? We believe all men are created equal. We know there are perfectly equal triangles and perfectly equal lines in geometric theory. Moreover, we never see in our physical universe two lines or two triangles that are perfectly equal. Where did the notion of equality come from if we cannot see it in our material world? Within the tri-unity of God, the Father, the Son, and the Holy Spirit were and are coequal. That is the unchanging basis that man has for equality among humankind. Humanity is created in the image and likeness of the Triune God; thus, we have an objective standard for equality. With Allah, can you justify unchanging equality?

Muslim: I have never thought of that.

Mike: One last thing. All men have sinned. You and I have broken God's law. God is perfect, and heaven is perfect. How can a sinner get into a perfect paradise? Only Jesus Christ has the solution in His atoning work on the cross. He died to rinse away the sins of His people, and true Christians have justification before heaven's court. That means my sins are taken away and Christ's perfect record of righteousness is imputed to me, credited to my spiritual account. Do you know if you died tonight whether you would go to heaven?

Muslim: No. I try my best. Can we get together? I would like you to come over my house and talk to me and my wife.

Mike: Yes, let me get your e-mail and phone number.

The Trinity Must Be

A solitary god would depend on men and angels to fulfill some inner lack. This unitarian god would lack love, communication, and equality in his essential nature and being. Without the attributes of love and fellowship he could not even be a personal being. If this solitary god needed to create angels, jinn, or men to give and receive love, that would imply that he depends on his creation. Love, fellowship, equality, and personhood are essential to God's being. Only the Biblical God has these attributes as essential to His being. God is God, and He does not depend on His creation for anything. Without people and cherubim, God would still love and have fellowship, and not lack anything. Francis Schaeffer rightly summed up the solution that the Trinity provides:

> The Nicene Creed—three persons, one God....Whether you realize it or not, that catapulted the Nicene Creed right into our century and its discussion: three Persons in existence, loving each other, and in communication with each other, before all else was. If this was not so, we would have had a God who needed the universe as much as the universe needed God. But God did not need to create; God does not need the universe as the universe needs Him. Why? God is a full and true Trinity. The Persons of the Trinity communicated with

each other before the creation of the world. This is not only an answer to the acute philosophic need of unity in diversity, but of personal unity and diversity. The unity and diversity cannot exist before God or behind God, because whatever is farthest back is God....The unity and diversity are in God Himself— three persons, yet one God....[T]his is not the best answer; it is the only answer. Nobody else, no philosophy, has ever given an answer for unity and diversity....Every philosophy has this problem, and no philosophy has an answer. Christianity does have an answer in the Trinity. The only answer to what exists is that He, the starting-place, is there.[7]

If the Triune God does not exist, then knowledge is impossible. That is a self-contradictory notion, and it is impossible because it is a knowledge claim. Only the Christian worldview supplies the foundation necessary for love, logic, science, moral standards, and mathematics. Non-Christian gods and systems of thought cannot furnish a foundation for the law of non-contradiction; therefore, those systems of thought can only offer a self-contradictory worldview. God in Trinity is the precondition for all knowledge, science, and logic. It is impossible for God not to exist, for He is the precondition for the intelligibility of the universe. The nonphysical, transcendent, and immutable God supplies the necessary preconditions for the use of the nonphysical, transcendent, universal, and immutable laws of logic. To argue at all, you must presuppose that the Triune God lives.

Non-Christian thought cannot supply the necessary preconditions for the laws of logic; thus, it is false. The contrary of the Trinity is impossible, and all non-Christian worldviews fall into absurdity because they cannot explain the universe and are self-contradictory. They lead to conclusions that contradict their own primary assumptions. Without the one God—the Father, the Son, and the Holy Spirit—nothing can make sense. The true and living God is the precondition for knowledge and the understanding all of human experiences, including the problem of the one and the many. One God in three persons is the inescapable truth. He alone provides the preconditions for the universal and unchanging laws of logic. Universal claims for truth are inescapable. The Christian God alone provides the preconditions for universal claims; hence Christianity must be true.

The grace of the Lord Jesus Christ, and the love of God, and the communion of the Holy Spirit, be with you all. Amen (2 Corinthians 13:14).

Notes

[1] Julian Huxley, *Religion without Revelation* (New York: Mentor Books, 1957), p. 45.

[2] Walter Kaufmann, *Critique of Religion and Philosophy* (Garden City, NY: Anchor Books, 1961), p. 127.

[3] John Gerstner, *Theology in Dialogue* (Morgan, PA: Soli Deo Gloria, 1996), p. 42.

[4] John A. T. Robinson, *Honest to God* (Philadelphia: Westminster Press, 1963), p. 64.

[5] John M. Frame, *Apologetics to the Glory of God* (Phillipsburg, NJ: P & R, 1994), pp. 40-50.

[6] John Muether, *So Great a Salvation* (Philadelphia: Modern Reformation Vol. 10, No. 3. May/June 2001), p. 8.

[7] Francis Schaeffer, *Trilogy: He Is There and He Is Not Silent* (Westchester, IL: Crossway, 1990), pp. 288-289.

CHAPTER EIGHT

THE LONG STARE OF A HOLY GOD

Sartre claimed that he became an atheist because a man stared at him in public. He felt uncomfortable and dehumanized by becoming an object of the long stare of a stranger. He then reasoned: God is omnipresent, hence God must have His eyes perpetually on Sartre. But he did not like God gazing at him. Thus he denied God because of his quirky shyness. God is present everywhere and looks upon everyone always. God sees all the iniquity of mankind, and we should remind people of that fact.

The bombastic atheist Madalyn Murray O'Hair and her two atheist grandchildren were murdered in a horrible fashion. She was forced to watch her grandchildren be tortured to death by a fellow-atheist who had stolen their organization's monetary assets. O'Hair was the cantankerous lady who lifted up and shook her deviant fist and yelled at God, "I don't believe in you; I reject you." If she did not believe in God, at whom was she yelling? She knew God was there. And now that she is deceased, she surely knows. Yet sadly, because of her worldview, she could not morally argue against her attacker for torturing her and her loved ones. An atheistic worldview cannot assert an objective and unchanging morality. Murder should be looked on as a good thing in the atheist worldview. If their creed is survival of the fittest, then those who murder are more fit than their victims. Therefore, the atheist cannot say that murder is wrong. If anything, they should delight in the killing of weaker members of an evolving species. The species is progressing through natural selection by the hands of murderers, which will provide a stouter gene pool for the ascent of the species. Christians can justify their outrage at murder and proclaim in a consistent manner that all murder is morally wrong. We do this through God's holy law. No other worldview can assert that murder is universally, unalterably, and objectively evil and remain consistent. Christianity is the precondition for morality and ethics, including the forbidding of murder.

Many unbelievers have complained about my use of the words "hell" and "repent." Frequently they are repulsed by such words. They do not have much of a problem with the mush of the ultra-tolerant, decaffeinated, warm, and fuzzy modern religion. But they are very much discomforted by the believer who warns them about the wrath to come. They tell me that it is distasteful to use fear as a way to motivate people to become Christians. The salty atheist Bertrand Russell declared: "Religion is based, I think, primarily and mainly upon fear."1 Since this dogmatic declaration is from an atheist, it can be turned back upon him. I would respond to this accusation by asserting that the atheist is afraid of hell, and due to his fear tries to deny the unpleasant reality of hell. He builds his worldview primarily upon fear, the fear of a real hell. He acts like a philosophical ostrich, sticking his head in the sand, hoping the truth of hell will just go away by his denying its reality. My faith is built on love and a respectful fear of a Holy God. The hell denier lives in fear—the fear of hell. He is passionate when the subject is brought up, because he knows it is true. Thus he suppresses the truth in unrighteousness and hopes hell will just go away. He lives and moves in fear of hell. Hell is real, and so is heaven. Everyone will spend eternity in one of those two places. Henry Buckle wrote: "If immortality be untrue, it matters little whether anything else be true or not." That is how important eternity is. If there is eternal life, then that truth is one of the most important issues with which people must deal with. This should motivate the unbeliever to come to Christ and compel the believer to share his faith.

If we say that we have no sin, we deceive ourselves, and the truth is not in us (1 John 1:8).

Christianity: The Only Place Where Justice and Grace Meet

If I receive a speeding ticket, go to court, and the judge asks, "What do you plead?" and I say, "Guilty, but I promise I will never speed again. Judge, please forgive my ticket on account of my future obedience," the judge would say, "It is good that you will not speed again. That is your lawful duty. But you still have to pay the fine for your past mistake of speeding." The good news is that Jesus Christ, as judge, came down, took off His robe, and paid the fine Himself for all who trust in Him.

All thirty thousand religions, except one, believe that your future good works will help you get to heaven, nirvana, freedom from the karmic cycle, or paradise. Yet our good deeds can never erase our bad deeds. If I murder nine people and later help feed ten thousand people at a shelter, I am still a murderer. If caught and tried, the good works will not rinse away my capital crimes. We all have sinned. The unbeliever tries to deny this truth. John Piper reminds us of this by stating that "God warns with His wrath and woos with His kindness." The atonement expiates the sins of the Christian and rinses his transgressions from his spiritual record. Then God graciously imputes Christ's righteousness to the believer's account. We enter heaven free from past sins and clothed in the righteousness of Christ through faith alone and by grace alone.

To you first, God, having raised up His servant Jesus, sent Him to bless you, in turning away every one of you from your iniquities (Acts 3:26).

Life Is Like a Vapor

Every person you will ever see will die one day and face a Holy God. Homer put it this way in the *Iliad*: "Death in ten thousand shapes hangs ever over our heads, and no man can elude him." One thing that all of us have in common is that we will all die. The clerk at the corner store, your neighbor, your family, and your friends will all die. My exhortation to you is: Ponder the realities of hell; remember, hell and eternity always seem to go together in the Bible.

Knowing, therefore, the terror of the Lord, we persuade men (2 Corinthians 5:11).

The evangelist Ray Comfort describes the time he "approached a young man who was using a string of profanities....I asked him to try the I.Q. test (a test on a tract that exposes the sinner's law breaking). He said he had told a few white lies, lifted things here and there, and of course lusted. When I gently said that God saw him as a lying, thieving adulterer at heart, his eyes widened, and he used the name of Jesus in blasphemy, to which I replied, 'And a blasphemer!' He looked horrified and exclaimed, 'G-d.' I said, 'Twice over!' He then put his hand on his mouth and muttered, 'You make me feel like going to confession. I'm so embarrassed!' Conscience did its duty. He did not need a priest; he needed a Savior"[2] The law is a supernatural tool that breaks down our pride. God, by His grace, breaks up the fallow ground of the most hardened heart through the power of His holy word. We all need Jesus.

Go and Tell

And when He got into the boat, he that had been demon-possessed begged Him that he might be with Him. However, Jesus did not permit him, but said to him, "Go home to your friends, and tell them what great things the Lord has done for you, and how He has had compassion on you." And he departed and began to proclaim in Decapolis all that Jesus had done for him; and all marveled (Mark 5:18-20).

In this passage Jesus commands a formerly possessed man to go and tell others of the great things God has done. One of the first witnesses for Christ was not a seminary graduate, nor an expert in apologetics, nor a close disciple, nor an expert in theology. It was neither John nor Paul; Jesus found his first witness in a cemetery. He was a graveyard lunatic, an ancient Charles Manson. He cut himself with rock—a form of Satan worship in antiquity. This cemetery dweller must have been like Ted Bundy, Jeffrey Dahmer, David Berkowitz, and Tex Watson: all mass murderers who professed faith in Christ after being imprisoned for capital crimes. This graveyard crazy was an unlikely witness until he met Jesus. If he could go and tell others about the glories of God in Christ, certainly we can. The statistics on death are impressive: Two hundred and forty people die every hour of every day, and most of them die without Jesus. The woman at the well had a troubled past and made a mess of her marriages. She came to Jesus, and God saved her. Jesus then sent her to tell her hometown about Him. If she could tell the lost about the Lord, we can be a witness. The mission of every believer is to pass on to others what we have received from Jesus. Witnessing is part of our earthly warfare.

As he looks at reality, the non-Christian uses a different foundational lens than the Christian. The non-Christian is like Lord Nelson, who, whenever a communication signal was flashed before him that he wanted to disregard, would put his telescope to his blind eye and say, "I really do not see the signal." This is how the unbeliever lives. He does not want to see the signal of God's revelation that he is a lost and doomed sinner. He wishes to suppress the truth of Christianity. He does not want to embrace Christianity's consistent presuppositions, so he tries to put the lens of God's revelation on his blind eye. He wants to evade the truth, suppress the truth, and disregard the truth. He whistles in the dark, hoping to avoid the unpleasant task of facing the reality of God's revelation in Christ Jesus. This is impossible.

Justification: Declared Righteous

Clouds and darkness surround Him: righteousness and justice are the foundation of His throne (Psalms 97:2).

[M]ercy triumphs over judgment (James 2:13).

Therefore, having been justified by faith, we have peace with God through our Lord Jesus Christ....For when we were still without strength, in due time Christ died for the ungodly. For scarcely for a righteous man will one die; yet perhaps for a good man someone would even dare to die. But God demonstrates His own love toward us, in that while we were still sinners, Christ died for us. Much more then, having now been justified by His blood, we shall be saved from wrath through Him (Romans 5:1-9).

Justification is a doctrinal term. The doctrine is laid out in the books of Romans and 1 Corinthians, among others. Justification as a doctrine is unique to Christianity. The doctrine of justification holds that the believer is declared righteous, his sins are removed, and Christ's righteousness is imputed unto him by faith in and the grace of Christ alone. No other religious system has a means by which to erase our record of iniquity and grant us a righteous record, so that we can enter a perfect heaven. Justification is a legal, forensic term that implies prior condemnation and results in pardon.

In 2001, when the Chinese held American servicemen and their aircraft captive, China demanded a legal apology from the United States government. The Chinese told the world that the U.S. aircraft was an illegal spy plane that purposely downed a Chinese jet. They told the American government that they wouldn't release our servicemen and women without an apology. China had sent the aggressive pilot to clip our plane, and he died due to his own aggressive actions. Yet China, a nation that never apologizes, demanded and received an apology. During the negotiation for this legal "I'm sorry," the U.S. government discovered that the Chinese have three types of apologies. *Yi Hah* is a mild, ambiguous apology that means "I wished it hadn't happened." *Bao Qian* is a more serious form of "I'm sorry," usually accompanied with a bow. *Dao Qian* is a forensic, legal, and formal apology, in which the speaker accepts full responsibility for his actions. *Dao Qian* is the strongest version of an apology. This is what China demanded from the American government—a legal and formal apology. In the same manner, the holy God of the universe demands a formal, forensic righteousness, not because He is capriciously harsh but because He is completely righteous. God is not arbitrary; He is holy and perfect. One must be righteous to live with Him in heaven. Every man has broken God's holy law; the only solution for man's sin and depravity is a formal, legal justification through Christ by grace through faith.

> But to him who does not work, but believes on Him who justifies the ungodly, his faith is counted for righteousness (Romans 4:5).

Most Christians understand that, because Christ died on the cross, their sins are forgiven and rinsed away; this is the negative aspect of justification. Something is subtracted, namely our sins. The positive aspect of justification is usually overlooked by the average modern Christian. The positive element of justification states that God imputes into the believer's account the righteousness of Christ. Jesus not only died for us; He lived for us. His perfect, holy, and righteous life was given to those who trust in Him. Christians know that Jesus atoned for their sins and disobedience on the cross, but His work was not merely negative and passive. During His life of thirty-three years, Jesus lived in perfect accord with God's law, fulfilling all righteousness on our behalf. Saved believers stand perfectly righteous before the Holy God. They are not just guiltless and sinless, but they are actually declared righteous on account of Christ. All that Jesus did on the earth is imputed into the believer's account. We are justified before God through the active and passive obedience of Jesus. We are saved by His life and His death; that is good news. Only Christianity can bestow justification. All the world's other religions are based upon the religionist's good deeds and personal merit. The problem is that heaven is perfect, God is holy, and nothing unholy and unrighteous will enter God's heaven. Biblical justification is the only solution to man's sin and Adam's disobedience.

The Eternal Blessing of Imputation

And he believed in the LORD; and He accounted it to him for righteousness (Genesis 15:6).

Therefore, having been justified by faith, we have peace with God through our Lord Jesus Christ (Romans 5:1).

For they have healed the hurt of the daughter of My people slightly, saying, Peace, peace; when there is no peace (Jeremiah 8:11).

Justification forensically renders the believer righteous and gives him peace with heaven. Without justification, the unbeliever has no peace with God. We must never assert that there is peace when there is no peace between the ungodly and God. Without justification by grace alone, there can be no real peace. "Imputation" is the Biblical term for the positive element of justification. Through God's grace by faith, the believer is declared righteous. Christ preached: "Be perfect, even as your heavenly Father is perfect" (Matthew 5:48). The law demands perfect obedience—a perfection equal to the Father's perfection. Nobody except Christ has accomplished this, so we need a perfect righteousness that is not our own. We need to be justified by the works and righteousness of another. Justification is a forensic term which speaks of the Christian's legal position before God. The believer is declared righteous despite his unrighteous deeds.

The justified are given an alien righteousness, a righteousness that is not their own but is imputed unto them by faith. Not having a righteousness of our own ensures that God gets all the glory. As Thomas Boston puts it, "We cry down the law when it comes to our justification, but we set it up when it comes to our sanctification. The Law drives us to the Gospel that we are Justified, then sends us to the Law again to show us our duty now that we are justified."

Share What You Have

He who continually goes forth weeping, bearing seed for sowing, shall doubtless come again with rejoicing, bringing his sheaves with him (Psalms 126:6).

In 1940 a butterfly collector was in Utah trying to enlarge his collection of bugs. At dusk he returned from his excursion and shared with his companion that he had heard a loud moaning and a cry for help. Someone was calling for assistance down the stream. His friend asked him whether he stopped and looked for the man who was in trouble. He said, "No, I had to get a particular butterfly." The next morning the corpse of a gold prospector was discovered in what later was named Dead Man's Gulch. Are we like the indolent butterfly collector? People are all around us, dying in their sins, and we are too busy or too dull to reach out to help. Is your life a spiritual Dead Man's Gulch or is it a lifesaving station? I want to care like George Whitefield cared when he pleaded, "Weep out, if possible, every argument, and compel them to cry, 'Behold, how He loves us.'" A long time ago, I decided I didn't want the sum of my life to be just a lot of stuff in storage and zeroes in a money market account. I discovered I wanted my life to count for eternity. I wanted to share what He freely gave me in Christ.

A Call for a Renewed Spirit of Sacrifice

History records that legions of Christians made great sacrifices for their faith in the first few centuries after Christ's resurrection and later during the Reformation. Today millions of Christians are suffering for their faith in Muslim countries, China, and North Korea. Western Christians have become soft. If we are honest, we would admit that we tend to have a greater passion for the Internet and television than we do for the lost; we are all guilty of this. Too often our lives revolve around our fun fixes and quests for pleasure. I am convicted by these words of Ignatious of Antioch:

> *I am God's wheat.*
> *May I be ground by the teeth of the wild beasts,*
> *Until I become the fine white bread that*
> *belongs to Christ.*

A Small Thing Can Lead to Big Things

The Scottish missionary Robert Moffat came home to England from his mission in South Africa to help recruit more missionaries. He arrived at the small church to teach and noticed only a few people had shown up to hear him speak and most of these were women. He was very disappointed in the turnout. He tried not to let it bother him and he preached his text from Proverbs 8:4: "Unto you, O men, I call." In his disappointment, he almost failed to notice a little boy in the back. Moffat felt hopeless as he preached his sermon, because he figured the jungles would be too challenging for any of the ladies to join up as missionaries. But God is God; He frequently works in ways we do not understand. No one signed up that night, but that little boy in the back was thrilled by the call and the challenge and decided to follow that pioneer missionary when he finished school. After graduation the boy, whose name was David Livingston, became one of the most successful missionaries in the history of African missions. We may never know in this world all the people we touched and radically changed through God's word; they may be the next successful missionaries or preachers.

My main purpose in writing this book was to glorify the Triune God and persuade Christians to share their faith. I identify with the great Russian novelist Fyodor Dostoevsky, who wrote these rallying words: "Sometimes, even if he has to do it alone and his conduct seems crazy, a man must set out an example and so draw men's souls out of their solitude, and spur them to some great act of brotherly love, that the great idea may not die."

Louis XIV ruled as king of France for a record seventy-two years, the longest in European history. He grew in power with great kingly strength and a huge realm. He declared that he was the state. Yet in 1715 he left the throne. He died. His funeral was spectacular, with a solid gold coffin and all the pomp and ceremony of a majestic ruler— thousands and thousands of mourners and only one lit candle signifying his greatness. At the appointed time in the funeral the minister stood to address the crowd. When he rose he did something that stunned the nation. Bending down, he snuffed out the lone candle representing the late king's greatness. The people gasped. Then came just four words from behind an open Bible: "Only God is Great."

The Puritan Ralph Venning discusses the righteousness of God in his book *The Sinfulness of Sin*. He says: "God is holy, without spot or blemish, or any such thing, without wrinkle, or anything like it....He is holy, that He cannot sin himself....He is without iniquity, and of purer eyes than to behold iniquity....God is holy, all holy, only holy, altogether holy." Our sin is real and God's holiness is pure and true. The only way one enters His perfect heaven is in perfect holiness; no man has that. We need our sins removed and replaced with a perfect righteousness. This is what God demands and God supplies when one puts his faith in Christ. God does exist and He did send His Son to die for His people. The contrary is impossible. The truth of the Gospel is that you must put all your trust in Jesus Christ and His atoning death and resurrection.

Give Away What You Have Received: Steps to Be A Witness

Turn from your will and trust in Christ. Believe the Gospel and be saved.

Pray. Ask God for a holy zeal for the lost.

Plan. Scratch out a specific time on your calendar to go out and evangelize.

Prepare. Pick up some tracts, a note pad, and a pen.

Partner. Call a friend in advance to go out with you.

Preach. Step out and go to hand out tracts in the marketplace.

Pray. Pray for the lost to come to Christ. Pray daily for a passion to witness to your neighbors, coworkers, store clerks, and everyone you see in your personal routine.

Go therefore and make disciples of all the nations, baptizing them in the name of the Father, and of the Son, and of the Holy Spirit: teaching them to observe all things that I have commanded you; and lo, I am with you always, even to the end of the age. Amen (Matthew 28:19-20).

Notes

[1] Bertrand Russell, *Why I Am Not A Christian* (New York: Simon & Schuster, 1964), p. 22.

[2] Ray Comfort, *The Ten Commandments* (Bellflower, CA: Living Waters, 1993), pp. 174-175.